HOMILIES FOR THE CELEBRATION OF MARRIAGE

Homilies for the Celebration of Marriage

by
A. M. Roguet O.P.

Translated by
Jerome J. DuCharme

Franciscan Herald Press
1434 W. 51st Street • Chicago, Ill. 60609

Homilies for the Celebration of Marriage by A. Roguet, translated by Jerome J. DuCharme from the original French, *Homelies pour le mariage pour le bapteme*, Editions Salvator, Mulhouse 1975. Copyright © 1977 by Franciscan Herald Press, 1434 West 51st Street, Chicago, Illinois 60609.

Library of Congress Cataloging in Publication Data

Roguet, A   M   1906–
    Homilies for the celebration of marriage.

    Translation of Homélies pour le mariage.
    Includes readings pertaining to marriage from the
1969 Lectionary.
    1. Wedding sermons. 2. Catholic Church—Sermons.
3. Sermons, English—Translations from French.
4. Sermons, French—Translation into English.
I. Catholic Church. Liturgy and ritual. Lectionary
(1969, English, U.S.). Marriage. 1977. II. Title.
BV4278.R6313   252'.1   76-53538
ISBN 0-8199-0656-5

Published with Ecclesiastical Approval

MADE IN THE UNITED STATES OF AMERICA

ABBREVIATIONS

Old Testament

Gn	Genesis	Eccl	Ecclesiastes
Ex	Exodus	Song	Song of Songs
Nm	Numbers	Wis	Wisdom
Dt	Deuteronomy	Sir	Sirach
Jos	Joshua	Is	Isaiah
Jgs	Judges	Jer	Jeremiah
1 Sm	1 Samuel	Bar	Baruch
2 Sm	2 Samuel	Ez	Ezechiel
1 Kgs	1 Kings	Dn	Daniel
2 Kgs	2 Kings	Am	Amos
Neh	Nehemiah	Mi	Micah
Tb	Tobit	Hb	Habakkuk
2 Mc	2 Maccabees	Zep	Zephaniah
Ps	Psalms	Zech	Zechariah

New Testament

Mt	Matthew	Col	Colossians
Mk	Mark	1 Thes	1 Thessalonians
Lk	Luke	2 Thes	2 Thessalonians
Jn	John	1 Tm	1 Timothy
Acts	Acts of the	2 Tm	2 Timothy
	Apostles	Ti	Titus
Rom	Romans	Phlm	Philemon
1 Cor	1 Corinthians	Heb	Hebrews
2 Cor	2 Corinthians	1 Jn	1 John
Gal	Galatians	Rv	Revelation
Eph	Ephesians		(Apocalypse)
Phil	Philippians		

Contents

READINGS FROM THE FOUR GOSPELS

INTRODUCTION

OPTIONAL READINGS

After Father Gonzague Motte completed his three volumes of homilies for Sundays in cycles A, B, and C,[1] he gave some thought to writing another series that would correspond to the lectionaries for marriage, baptism for children, and funerals. But his death prevented him from undertaking this task and no one was able to find any notes on the subject among his papers. His editors invited me to write the series in his place, and it was only with hesitation that I agreed to accept this task, which presented a new challenge.

The *Lectionary for Sundays and Feasts* determines the arrangement of the three readings. The preacher has ample material from which to choose the points he will comment on, until he finally decides the point of departure in his homily. The "ritual" lectionaries are different. They propose an "à la carte" menu, if we may use such terminology. The readings are independent. In the marriage liturgy, for example, there are ten optional gospels, each of which can be preceded in an *ad lib* manner by one of eight Old Testament readings or by one of ten readings from the New Testament. There can be even more combinations if three readings are used, as in the Liturgy of the Word for a feast day. We have to rely on mathematicians to give us the number of possible combinations between these two (or three) series of elements.

It is therefore impossible to present homilies that are developed in their entirety. Each reading will have an independent commentary.

1. Published in English in three volumes: *Homilies for Sundays of the Year* (Cycles A, B, and C) (Chicago: Franciscan Herald Press).

A PRACTICAL NOTE

The Scripture readings have not been reproduced, because the lectionary may be consulted; however, our commentary follows the exact order of the readings as they appear in the lectionary.

The italicized, unquoted words in our text are citations from the reading that is being considered. All other biblical citations are in regular print, in quotes, and are followed by their exact reference.

Each reading is designated by the number it carries in the official English lectionary that is used in the celebration of the sacrament.

For *Homilies for the Celebration of Marriage,* we then printed the title and the biblical reference from the lectionary.[1] Quite often our commentary is prefaced by two or three paragraphs of introductory remarks that can be helpful in selecting and understanding the text. These introductory remarks, however, are not intended for public reading.

For *Homilies for the Celebration of Baptism for Children,* we give the number and the biblical reference from the lectionary, then a title that we think is appropriate.

1. Translator's note: Instead of reproducing the equivalent titles from the English lectionary, I translated the author's French titles.

MARRIAGE AND OTHER SUBJECTS

The readings for marriage present a difficulty that does not occur in the series for the other two sacraments. Most of the readings in the baptismal lectionary deal directly with baptism; all the readings of the funeral liturgy make reference to death. Paradoxically, of the twenty eight readings proposed for marriage, only twelve are directly concerned with the union of man and woman. Certainly this "great mystery" is present throughout the Bible. But that number is not enough to furnish a significant number of readings fit for liturgical use, and several explanations may be given.

First, scattered allusions do not come together to form a consistent reading. Another explanation is that marriage is presented as an image or symbol, rather than in its human and truly sacramental reality. (That is why, in our opinion, the text from the book of Revelation will rarely be used.) Another reason for the rarity of texts that directly relate to marriage is in the fact that the theme of marriage is at times associated with adultery and prostitution, as in Hosea 1 and 2 and Ezekiel 16. Furthermore, the Bible occasionally compares the married state to celibacy and virginity, as in the First Letter to the Corinthians. It is easy to understand that the reading of such texts at a nuptial celebration would be in poor taste.

There is no difficulty with the twelve texts that pertain directly to marriage; but what about the other sixteen readings? They are of two kinds. Some readings are like a panoramic reminder of God's plan and the Christian ideal. Examples are the new covenant, foretold in Jeremiah 31; the Beatitudes; the parables of salt and light; and the parable of the house built on rock. It is quite evident that the sacrament of marriage is inscribed in the economy of God's plan. Moreover, marriage frequently offers the occasion, or rather the grace, of a new conversion to Christian life. A reminder of the fundamental laws of God can be timely, especially if such a reading is complemented by another text that refers more specifically to marriage.

The second kind of marriage reading deals with *agape,* which signifies supernatural charity or love. (There are several readings in this category: numbers 1, 2, 4, 6, 8, and 9 in the New Testament readings and 5, 8, 9, and 10 among the gospels.) It is good to be reminded of Christ's great commandment at the time of embarking on a new phase in life. Besides, isn't marriage the sacrament of love? The only problem here, and we should not overlook it, is the necessity to make our vocabulary very precise. Christian love, *agape,* must not be confused with love in the common or ambiguous sense of the word.

THE HOMILY

That brings us to our final difficulty. It is especially familiar to priests who will want to use our commentaries— as will usually be the case—to celebrate the marriage of people with whom the priest is not well acquainted. The priest may even question whether the people who are being married have any spirituality whatever. In that light, don't the texts and commentaries we offer appear to be excessive, idealistic, and even utopian? That is possible. Nevertheless, we have to take a few considerations into account.

First of all, the perfection of charity must not be regarded as an ideal reserved for an elite group of Christians. The Second Vatican Council reminded us that everyone who believes in Christ is called to sanctity and therefore to the perfection of charity (the dogmatic *Constitution on the Church,* "Lumen Gentium," chap. V).

Furthermore, the vocation to marriage, the grace already attached to the desire for the sacrament, and the

14

emotion that normally accompanies such a major decision all converge to open hearts to a complete and generous pursuit of the Christian life. All the people in attendance may not be so touched, but at least we can hope to reach the bride and groom, to whom we primarily address our homily.

Finally, we should recognize that the liturgical reform, decided by the Council, has profoundly changed the manner of preaching at a wedding. In the past, the priest presided at the conclusion of a contract, which was followed by the blessing of the rings and a short prayer. The old ritual had been passed on from a Christian era in which the priest acted as a delegate of civil authority. If the priest had anything to say, he said it before the celebration as a kind of "allocution," which often took a worldly twist. The Mass followed all this, to complete the ceremony. But now the celebration of marriage is incorporated in the Mass, or at least in the "celebration of the Word." Preaching, therefore, takes on the character of a homily, closely linked with the Scripture texts that have just been read. This makes it clear to everyone that the celebration of marriage is situated at the heart of the Christian mystery.

There is no doubt that each homilist will have to use his pastoral sensitivity and his talent for adaptation to enrich the specific details to meet the needs and circumstances of the bride and groom. The homilist will recognize the need to modify or simplify the texts, which we explain to the best of our ability but necessarily in an *a priori* context.

OLD TESTAMENT READINGS

1. THE CREATION OF MAN AND WOMAN
(Gn 1:26–28, 31)

It is evident that this reading and the next (Gn 2: 18–24) are fundamental to the Christian doctrine of marriage. The two texts are also quoted several times in other readings. Perhaps it can be helpful to note these quotations so as to avoid repetition and to emphasize the unity of the two Testaments. Genesis 1:27 is cited in Readings from the Four Gospels, nos. 4 and 6 (Mt 19:4, Mk 10:6). Genesis 2:24 is quoted in the same gospels (Mt 19:5, Mk 10:7–8) and also in another New Testament reading, Eph 5:31.

It would seem logical that the use of these two Genesis readings would be apropos for every marriage; nevertheless, there are some problems. Each reading is but a fragment from a very extensive narrative. To explain the reading, we must place it in its context. But for many listeners that context is, in effect, a source of amusement. People imagine strange things when we mention the six days of creation, the animals God formed from dust, Adam's rib, etc. Because we are addressing people of an advanced technological culture, we should not take the risk of having them listen to inspired texts with a condescending attitude. These passages contain very important doctrine and must not be regarded as stories that only small children can appreciate. Because they have several figures of speech, our listeners must not be allowed to think that every statement is subject to contradiction by scientific findings.

The homilist will keep in mind that the two passages are quite independent. (We have also noted this in our commentary.) The reading from the first chapter of Genesis is in fact more recent (it comes from a "priestly" writing in the sixth century before Christ.) Genesis 2: 18–24 is more ancient (from the "Yahwistic" tradition of the tenth century B.C.). The first reading is much drier and more abstract, while the second is filled with imagery.

The imagery makes the second reading more difficult for our modern mentality.

We are celebrating a marriage, which is another way of saying the start of a new life, the beginning of an adventure toward the future. And so you may wonder why I would decide to explain to you a page at the very beginning of the first book of the Bible. This is the page that gives us the report of the appearance of man on earth, which occurred, according to various scientific estimates, at least 50,000 and perhaps 500,000 years ago.[1]

The person who wrote the final version of this section of Genesis was an ancient Hebrew priest in the sixth century before Christ.[2] How strange if his intention had been to narrate how these events occurred in an age so distant from him! But that was not his purpose. He makes no scientific pretense but gives only a human and religious perspective on what, in his own words, happened *in the beginning,* which is still current for us. This "beginning" belongs also to us, and enlightens us not only about our origin but, even more importantly, about our nature, our destiny, and our vocation.

A few moments ago we were told that God created heaven and earth, the light, the waters, vegetation, the stars, and the animals. All of this happened at God's command. Everything was created by a simple word. But on the sixth day of this week of work was a more important creation that will crown all the rest. It seems that God reflects and encourages himself: *Let us make man.* But we are told nothing about the manner in which man is made. Instead, the passage instructs us on the vocation of this superior creature: *Let us make man in our image, after our likeness. Let them have dominion over . . . all*

1. See J. De Fraine, *The Bible and the Origin of Man* (New York, 1962, p. 12.

2. See H. Cazelles in the revised edition of *Introduction à la Bible* (Tournai, 1973), 2:231.

the creatures that crawl on the ground. Thus we learn the manner in which man is created in God's likeness, insofar as he receives power from God over the rest of creation. God will tell him in the next moment: *Subdue the earth.* Man is defined as God's steward, entrusted with managing and even continuing God's creation. The grandeur of science and technology finds its basis in that brief biblical phrase.

God effectively realizes his plan: *God created man in his image.* But now we are given more information about how God's image would be realized: *Male and female he created them.* The division of the human race into two sexes, therefore, is not of secondary importance. Sexual differences are not the result of a regrettable accident or the consequence of a punishment, as some mythologies, far removed from Christine doctrine, have conjured up. It is essential that humanity be male and female. Humanity is fully realized or developed only in the complementary union of man and woman. In the truest sense, they are "made for each other." In the beginning, God created the human race *male and female.* It is only in sexual diversity, which reflects some of God's richness and goodness, that we are able to say that humanity is indeed created in God's image. *God blessed them* signifies that he congratulated them and promised them happiness.

There is also another way in which the new creatures are privileged to resemble God: *Be fertile and multiply.* Man and woman are oriented toward children. Their union, their unity, is called a multiplying. They share in creation in that they themselves become procreators. It is true, however, that the previous verses of the Genesis narrative told us that God had already blessed the animals and had said to them: *Be fertile and multiply,* and that man, by his carnal nature, is a cousin to the animals. Human reproduction and multiplying, however, are far more dignified, because man and woman give birth to children who, in resembling their parents, bear the likeness of God (see Gn 5:3).

After each work of creation the author repeats: *God*

saw how good it was. After the creation of man, the verse concludes with *God looked at everything he had made, and he found it very good.* The description *very good* is surely accorded to creation in its entirety (*everything he had made*), but *very good* also pertains to the summit of creation, God's masterpiece: humanity, both male and female.

What follows in the Bible shows us how creation became tainted by sin; we hear accounts of many crimes, wars, and calamities of every kind. Nonetheless, the very first page of the Bible gives us a fundamental conviction that we must never abandon: Whatever happens, the world is basically good; life is good; marriage is good.

If you yourselves did not have such a conviction, would you be here? Your certitude, however, must not flow from a careless and misguided optimism. We must not rely on the loose and facile hope that expects everyone to live "happily ever after." The opposite opinion, which considers nothing to be of value, should also be rejected.

As Christian optimists, we do not close our eyes to evil. We rely on the certainty of that truth about which this first page of the Bible has reminded us with force and simplicity: God, who is love, has placed us on earth so that we might govern this world, which is his creation. We accept our task in order to make creation better and more beautiful and so that we may continue to grow in the image and likeness of him who has created us for happiness.

2. THE CREATION OF WOMAN
(Gn 2:18–24)

See the paragraphs that introduce the previous reading (p. 19).

You have just heard part of the most ancient account of creation that has come down to us. The passage makes no scientific pretense; so we would be making a grave mistake if we search the text for a treatise on natural history. Also, it would be as great an error to smile indulgently, as though we were listening to a fairy tale or a legend from folklore. This ancient, 3,000-year-old text uses a figurative style and gives us an unsophisticated narrative, understandable to the simplest minds, in order to reveal some very profound human and religious truths.

After God created man, who makes his appearance as a unique being, *God said: It is not good for the man to be alone. I will make a suitable partner for him.*" Our ancient author had often watched a potter fashion earthenware out of every form of clay, and so he portrays the act of creation as clay modeling. Then God leads the animals to man, and man names them. The "staging" of this story may appear infantile to us, but for anyone who knows the special significance of a name in the mentality of the ancient East, this "naive" scene has considerable meaning.

The first man is capable of giving names to the animals. This means that he knows them and that he is intelligent. Furthermore, knowing the name of a creature, especially a living creature, means possession of authority over that creature. Having the power to name it means to be able to make it "come forward," to be able to command and dominate it.

Again, therefore, we disciver what is mentioned in another account in Genesis, namely, that man is created in God's image and likeness. Like God, man dominates creation, although, of course, on a more modest level. The significance of the domination is twofold: man is superior to creation and he governs creation.

By possessing such deep knowledge of animals, man understands that he is of a completely different nature. That is why *none proved to be the suitable partner for the man.* God is about to give the man a female companion whom God will create especially for man by drawing her out of his substance.

This episode is well known and has provoked endless joking about "Adam's rib." However, the translation that was just read to you speaks, with complete fidelity to the original text, of Adam's *side,* which connotes his heart, and therefore his love. There is also an indication of the kind of companion the woman will be for man. She will live "at his side": God *brought her to the man.*

Why are we told that *the Lord God cast a deep sleep on the man?* Above all, we should not think that it refers to anesthesia, given in preparation for a surgical operation. The man's sleep was supernatural, for man cannot be a witness to God's work when that work is filled with such great mystery.

Yes, the origin of woman and the reciprocal inclination, which unites her to man, are profound mysteries that we must admire and respect as a work of God, a reflection of the love and care God shows to his creatures.

The same truth is again indicated to us by God's initiative, expressed in very simple and delicate terms: *God then made a woman . . . and brought her to the man.* Upon awakening, the man recognized her immediately, without having seen her before. With enthusiasm and gratitude, that is, with love, he discovers a being not only like him but of his very same nature, a being taken from him and made for him: *This one, at last, is bone of my bone and flesh of my flesh!* This expression, which is frequently used in biblical language, designates a being of the same race, who is so close, so alike, that there can be a mutual sharing of tastes and interests.

That is the biblical description of the creation of woman from man and man's enthusiastic discovery that the woman is his perfect partner. The narrator concludes: *That is why a man leaves his father and mother.* To establish a new home, man will have to detach himself from his original home and institute a new social unit, established on love and fidelity: he *clings to his wife, and the two of them become one body.* The Hebrew texts states literally: "The two will henceforth be but one flesh"; but it would be an error to retain that phrase. As often occurs in the Bible, the phrase in this passage has the precise

meaning of "one person only," "one being only." Surely
the union of man and woman is consummated in the flesh,
but the union goes beyond that: carnal union is both the
point of departure and the goal, the reality and the sign
of a union that encompasses one's entire being—body and
soul, heart and thoughts, life in its entirety—by which the
couple forms a unity, a unique home, united forever.

Therefore, only superficial minds will see these very
simple words and images as crude or childish. This page,
one of the first in the Bible, shows us thè vital role a
woman must fulfill for a man: to be a companion, a help-
er, a partner like unto him, equal to him in dignity.

3. THE MARRIAGE OF ISAAC
(Gn 24:48-51, 58–67)

This pericope was a late addition to the lectionary
for marriage. Indeed, "this Yahwistic narrative is the most
pleasant and charming of all the patriarchal stories," but
because "it exceeds the length of (most) Genesis narratives,"[3] it must be shortened considerably to produce an
acceptable liturgical reading. Although the English lectionary made some attempt to correct these mutilations
with a brief *incipit,* the abridgment made the narrative
less interesting and less charming. We are not told why
Abraham sent his servant into his native land. There is
total omission of the colorful scene at the spring, which
procures the sign that the servant had asked of God in
order to be assured that God had the situation well in
hand. Also omitted is the description of how Rebekah's
parents offered resistance to her immediate departure.

Also, these patriarchal customs, by which the choice
of a wife is made with complete disregard for the future,
are quite unlike our own customs.

Therefore it seems difficult to construct a true mar-

3. G. Von Rad, *Genesis* (rev. ed.; Philadelphia, 1972), p. 253.

riage homily on this mutilated text without running the risk of being esoteric. Taking all these considerations into account, we are content with offering some brief points of explanation.

The narrative of the marriage between Isaac and Rebekah, which comprised our first reading, may seem somewhat disconcerting. Isaac is not the one who asks to marry Rebekah; the request is made by an intermediary, Abraham's servant, to whom Abraham gave the responsibility of finding a wife for his sole heir in the distant land of his birth. In fact, Isaac and his father reside in Canaan, which will eventually be the Promised Land. But at that time, it was the land in which they had been exiled. All the potential wives that Isaac would have been able to find in Canaan were pagans.

The situation teaches us a useful lesson that is very adaptable to our own day and age. Marriage must not unite people who would remain divided because of their extremely unequal conditions in life. But if we admit, even more readily than did the contemporaries of Abraham, differences of wealth and even nationality, we should be much more willing to consider how these same differences might be offset by the profound harmony that results from the husband and wife's sharing a common outlook on life.

The narrative has another aspect that was almost completely hidden in the very brief version you have just heard: it is God who conducts our life. The same truth is stated in the old proverb "Marriages are made in heaven." Because Rebekah's parents recognized that God's intervention was a discrete intervention, which could be discovered only in the occurrence of ordinary events, they were resigned to Rebekah's hasty departure. That is also why the young girl was so ready to take the journey that would lead her to a man she did not know.

When they met, it was "love at first sight." The story

ends with these words: *He married her, she became his wife, and he loved her.*

According to the notions of romance that we are accustomed to, love comes before marriage—but the patriarchs of the Bible were not familiar with our popular novels. Nevertheless, their psychology was not as crude as it appears to us. And if, in our experience, marriage precedes love, can we not believe, and even wish, that marriage would be not only an end but a beginning as well and, with love crowning the marriage, that the relationship would become deeper and more solid?

4. THE MARRIAGE OF TOBIAH AND SARAH (TG 7:9c–10, 11c–17)

Because the book of Tobit's historical and geographical setting contains many errors and contradictions, it is the common opinion that the book is a fairy tale. Therefore nothing is accomplished in bringing up the book's historicity during a marriage celebration. The best approach is to present the two personalities as models with whom the husband and wife can easily identify.

By way of exception, the English text in the lectionary has been translated from the Vulgate, not from the original text, which is under discussion. We can question whether the original was Greek or Aramaic. With regard to the Vulgate, St. Jerome translated the book of Tobit in a single day. For his translation he used an Aramaic version and the "Old Latin" text. Jerome often shortened the text he was working on, or he developed it in such a way as to arrive at a meaning that gave edification to Christians. Most English Bibles follow the Greek text of Sinaiticus. The variances in the Vulgate correspond to the references in these English Bibles.

The Vulgate text offers liturgical and pastoral advantages. Only the Vulgate contains the intervention of Raphael, who commends Tobiah for his fidelity. Only the

Vulgate gives the benediction pronounced by Raguel (7: 15), which formed the Introit of the marriage Mass in the old Roman Missal. And only the Vulgate completes Tobiah's prayer with the invocation uttered by Sarah (8:10).

In the first reading from the book of Tobit you heard the story of a marriage. It is, clearly, a description of a Jewish marriage. The wedding was celebrated in a style quite different from the rustic customs that were observed in the time of the patriarchs, or in the time of Moses or David. The people of God have been purified and refined by the ordeal of the exile. The Jewish religion has become more delicate and more internalized, to such an extent that in reading the book of Tobit we sense a Christian atmosphere.

This does not mean that all these courageous people were steeped in devotion. They were normal people with normal desires; they had an intense love for life. In the reading, we heard how impatient Tobiah was to take Sarah for his wife. We were also told that after the marriage contract was signed, everyone sat down at a table to enjoy the wedding feast.

The people in our reading are faithful to God and aware of his protection as they live their very simple and spontaneous lives. Raguel, Sarah's father, hesitates to respond favorably to the young man's request for marriage. But the reason for his hesitation is that all the men who had previously had an interest in Sarah became victims of tragedy, undoubtedly because their intentions were not pure. The angel Raphael calms the father and assures him that there is nothing to fear with Tobiah, who is faithful to God. Then Raguel understands that Providence has arranged everything for the happiness of the young couple, whom God wants to bring together.

Raguel places the right hand of his daughter in Tobiah's hand. As was the custom in a patriarchal society, the father officiates at his daughter's wedding. He uses the magnificent formula that has often been repeated in the Christian liturgy of marriage: "May the God of Abraham, the God of Isaac, the God of Jacob be with you, and may he unite you and fill you with his blessings." Thus, though the symbolic action is performed by man, it is God himself who is at work. May he unite you. We might say that this believer, who lived several centuries before Christ, already saw marriage as a sacrament.

That is why it is easy for us to adopt the sentiments that inspired the participants in this scene. Hasn't today's groom really been led to his fiancée by the angel Raphael? Haven't your two families undergone the severe trials that occasioned the prayers of petition by Tobiah and Sarah, prayers that united them even at a distance? Even if you met in less extraordinary circumstances, your meeting was no less the work of Providence. You recognize this by the very fact that you have come here to be blessed by God and to have Christ be the privileged and sovereign authority of your union.

Therefore I take the words of the aged Raguel and adapt his words to this occasion: "May Christ the Lord be with you; may he unite you and fill you with his blessings."

5. THE PRAYER OF A YOUNG MARRIED COUPLE
(TG 8:5-10)

See the introductory note for the previous reading (p. 23).

The Old Testament passage, which we have just heard in the first reading, presented the young couple, Tobiah and Sarah, to us on their wedding night. Their refinement would edify many Christians of our day. At the very moment when they are to be united in love, they consecrate a time to prayer because they are conscious of being the descendants of a holy people.

What was true for the descendants of the patriarchs, who were loved by God, is even more true of the children of the Church. As baptized Christians, we belong to God's people, a people made holy by consecration and vocation, despite our weaknesses, even taking into consideration the faults of individuals, who make up the Church.

Like every true prayer—like the Lord's Prayer—Tobiah begins his prayer with his heart uplifted to God in thanksgiving: *Blessed are you, O God of our fathers; praised be your name forever and ever. Let the heavens and all your creation praise you forever.* Then Tobiah recalls the creation of the first man and woman, who made the first human marriage. Finally, he affirms that he has a religious intention in entering marriage: *Now, Lord, you know that I take this wife of mine not because of lust, but for a noble purpose.*

Let us be frank about it. We are embarrassed by one of the phrases in this beautiful profession of faith: *not because of lust, but for a noble purpose.* But if we understand the meaning of his words we see that Tobiah sets himself apart from Sarah's unfortunate suitors, who had been punished by God for wanting to marry *because of lust.* Tobiah enters marriage to obey God's law and to give God a long dynasty of faith-filled people.

However, that does not prevent him from loving Sarah with intensity. Throughout the passages that preceded today's reading we see how impatient Tobiah is to win the hand of the young girl. And how can we comprehend his impatience, except as a sign of love?

At the conclusion of Tobiah's prayer, his wife asks God for help. She is in complete agreement with the prayer offered by her husband. She, too, wishes to establish a family that would praise God forever. But because Tobiah has already expressed that desire, she does not repeat it. Her personal intervention is very touching; she sees only the two of them and the happiness they have in being together: *Allow us to live together to a happy old age.*

It is easy for the two of you to make the intentions of Tobiah and Sarah, who were married long ago, your own. Your relatives and friends, who have come here, have the same intentions. They wish to witness your happiness and to contribute to your happiness by their prayers. May God bless your union and see fit to *allow you to live together to a happy old age.*

6. LOVE IS AS STRONG AS DEATH
(Song 2:8–10, 14, 16c, 8:6–7a)

It frequently happens that this pericope is chosen by the engaged couple. There is nothing surprising about this, because the passage is a song about human love and therefore is easy to understand. It expresses incomparable poetic charm.

The reading, however, has certain drawbacks. Isn't it likely to give people who do not understand the Bible, or people who are "uptight" and easily scandalized, a reason to be surprised, amused, or scandalized? The homily must attempt to correct these reactions and, at the same time, place this text, or rather the entire Song of Songs, in its correct context. The context is the whole Bible, which contains the nuptial theme from cover to cover. That is the approach by which we have chosen to clarify the pericope.

We are familiar with the proliferation of diverse interpretations of the Song. For a long time, the allegorical interpretation was considered to be the original, based on the first rabbinic and patristic commentaries. The Song was written to evoke the love that united Yahweh to Israel. This position has been developed and systematized by A. Robert and A. Feuillet and by R. Tournay, who describe the meaning as a "geographic" allegory (the beloved is the Holy Land). These authors justify their opinion by referring to the many geographic allusions in the Bible.

The "anthological" style of the prophets especially supports this interpretation.

Opposed to the above viewpoint are the introductions to the Song in the single volume of the revised *La Bible de Jérusalem*, in *La Bible Osty*, and in W. Harrington's new *Introduction à la Bible* (pp. 454–460). These authors take the lead from articles by A. M. Dubarle and J. P. Audet and categorically refuse to attribute more to the Song than the literal meaning of a poem or a collection of poems, whose sole purpose is the musical portrayal of human love.

The latter opinion seems to us much too radical because it contradicts an interpretation without which we cannot understand why the Song was inserted in the biblical canon. Consequently, we would not be able to admit the presence of this book in the Bible, because it would have a purely profane purpose. Nor would we be able to consider this heterogeneous book to be inspired. But most important of all, the latter opinion seems to put too much restriction on the meaning of the word "literal." In a poetic book, particularly one that deals with love, we do not depart from the "literal" sense when we recognize resonances in the text that go beyond the letter.

The Song appears to us to be basically an exaltation of human love, but human love as the privileged symbol of God's love for his people. We believe we have accurately stated the position of H. Cazelles in his article "Cantique des cantiques" in the encyclopedia *Catholicisme* and in the new edition of *Introduction à la Bible* (2:607–610). Cazelles' position is also held by Pierre Grelot in his book *Man and Wife in Scripture*.

Some of you may have been surprised, if not shocked, to hear our first reading read in church, which is a very ardent dialogue of love, a dialogue that apparently has nothing to do with religion.

That is precisely the problem we find throughout the Song of Songs. Why is this small book given such prominence by being included in the Bible? It seems not to go beyond the horizons of human love, and mentions the name of God only once.[4]

Considered in its entirety, the Bible is both realistic and optimistic. The complete human condition has a proper place in the Bible. The Bible describes wars and betrayals, crimes and noble deeds. It tells several love stories[5] and emphasizes the physical beauty of David, Absalom, Esther, and Judith.

First of all, we have to say that in the Bible, love—human love—is something good, something willed by God as part of his plan. Human love contributes to the beauty of the world, which was created by God. We see the beginning of this perspective in the creation narrative, in the enthusiasm of the first man when he meets the woman who is destined to be his partner. The exclamation of the man, the lover in the Song, is not less expressive: *Arise, my beloved, my beautiful one, and come. . . . Let me see you, let me hear your voice!*

The love that a husband has for his wife is so noble that it is expressed from one end of the Bible to the other, throughout the Old and New Testaments—even in Revelation, the last book of the New Testament. The image of human love, the union between man and woman, is constantly used to evoke the mystery of the covenant, which is a kind of marriage: God's relationship with his people, Christ's relationship with the Church.

Such love is often described by the prophets in very, if not extremely, realistic terminology, as in the Song of Songs. But what makes the Song superior is its incomparable poetic charm. Everything takes place in spring-

---

4. The only exception is 8:6, which speaks of "a flash of fire, a flame of the Lord himself" (Jerusalem Bible translation). That is no more than a common expression indicating a superlative, just as those who use the expression "a thunderbolt from heaven" intend no religious connotation. The New American Bible translates the same phrase as "Its flames are a blazing fire."

5. For example, the love affairs of Jacob, Samson, David (criminal adultery), and Tobiah.

time, in the freshness of the early days of the world, amid perfumed fragrances and the singing of birds.

Therefore we are not considering an allegorical and intellectual love. And we are no longer considering, as at the beginning of the world, the meeting of the typical, original man (the meaning of Adam's name) and the woman whom God gave to him because "it is not good for the man to be alone" (Gn 2:18, Old Testament reading 2 in the lectionary for marriage). The Song describes a real adventure of love, a very personal kind of love between two individuals who have chosen each other. They are so unique to each other that in their eyes, it seems, the rest of humanity does not even exist.

The entire poem is a pursuit, a quest, a dialogue, an exchange of declarations, compliments, and outbursts of admiration and desire.

The reading, which you have just heard, is constructed by joining two brief passages together. Although the two sections are six chapters apart, their movement corresponds to the general flow of the book.

First, the young girl sees her beloved, coming to meet her, and recalls his words of love. The first section ends with a refrain that is repeated several times in the poem. It is like a slogan for the unity and the mutual nature of love: *My lover belongs to me and I to him.* When we hear this very simple and powerful expression, it is impossible not to think of the words of the prophets: "Israel will be my people, and I will be her God." We are also reminded of words that Jesus spoke to his disciples, such as "I am in my Father, and you in me, and I in you" (Jn 14:20).

Don't be surprised by this parallel between human love and divine love. Divine love is at the source of human love. Human love is like the projection on humanity of the love God has for us. Human love is also a pattern of the love we must have for God.

The second part of our reading is the husband's declaration of love. His words are rough, passionate, and violent. There is no question of a whimsical and fanciful love. This love is *as strong as death.* It is an indissoluble, indestructible love that indelibly engraves the names of the two lovers on their hearts.

Deep waters cannot quench love. The *deep waters* represent the trials of life. The enchantment of spring will not last forever. And you, in the course of years, will have to face difficulties, tragedies, and misunderstandings in your lives, and perhaps even in your relationship. But when love is real, and therefore blessed by God, *deep waters* cannot destroy it. Just the opposite is the case. Through the crises of life, love is strengthened.

Can we be honest about it? Our readings surprised you because there is a widespread prejudice that Christianity is the enemy of love. Christianity allegedly sees love as guilt ridden and, through the sacrament of marriage, tries to "excuse" it and make it less offensive. Nothing could be further from the truth.

Christianity is the religion of God's incarnate Son, who came in the flesh. Like its other source, the Bible, Christianity squarely faces the realities of love and the flesh. (Only deviations are condemned.) Christianity invites us to regard these realities as a work of God, a path that leads people to God. That is why human love, described briefly in the Song of Songs, will be sanctified and made indissoluble through the sacrament of love, through marriage, which you are now about to receive.

7. THE WIFE, LIGHT OF THE HOME
(Sir 26:1, 26:1–4, 16–21)

Let us begin by stating that the commentary we offer below can hardly pretend to constitute the outline of a consistent homily. It should also be stated that the charming text of Ben Sirach offers little input for the doctrine of marriage. Besides, will we be able to use this reading

very often in the celebration of marriage? Won't it be a
bit embarrassing for the bride to hear a description of
the portrait of the ideal wife?

Surely the homilist will prefer to stress the rich content of the gospels. However, the commentary that we
propose can help him understand this Old Testament
reading, to which he may wish to make references in the
homily.

Our short presentation of what the Bible tells us
about women takes several suggestions from H. Daniel
Rops' *Daily Life in the Time of Jesus* (New York, 1962),
pp. 148–153, and X. Leon-Dufour's *Dictionary of Biblical
Theology* (rev. ed.; New York, 1973), the article on woman.

The Old Testament could give us a rich repertory of
anti-feminist arguments and images. Its narratives present
us with a gallery of traitorous women, such as Delilah
(Jgs 16:4–26); vain women, such as Saul's daughter Michal,
who married David (2 Sm 6:20–23); or quarrelsome and
complaining women, such as the wife of Job (Jb 2:9–10)
and the wife of Tobit (Tb 2:11–14, 5:18–20). There are
impious and bloodthirsty queens, such as Jezebel (1 Kgs
19:1–2, 21:1–25) and Athaliah (2 Kgs 11). The Wisdom
books never run out of things to say about the faults and
dangerous qualities of women.

These somewhat bitter portrayals, however, have their
counterpart. The first reading, which we have just heard,
is a magnificent eulogy of the good wife, the courageous
and brave woman, gracious and full of talent. *A gift from
the Lord is her governed speech, and her firm virtue is
of surpassing worth.* (Nevertheless, it must be said, the
two parts of the eulogy are separated by a warning about
the wife who is jealous of another woman and the wife
who gossips and is immoral and immodest.) The ideal
wife, described in our reading, is an incomparable treasure.

Our eulogy of the perfect woman begins with the
beatitude: *Happy the husband of a good wife.* But in all

likelihood you have noticed that this beatitude emphasizes a limitation. The wife is praised only in relation to her husband and for the advantages she gives him. Her qualities seem somewhat passive: she knows when to be silent and when to be discreet. Indeed, these qualities hardly correspond to the feminist movement that is so popular today!

Even in the Old Testment, however, we find women who are active and very independent. The "strong woman," who is praised at the conclusion of the book of Proverbs, is a dominant woman, full of initiative. She is continually at work to increase the prosperity of her household.

It can be further noted that sacred history is filled with women who are national heroines, such as Jael (Jgs 4:17–23), Rahab (Jos 2:1–21, 6:17, 22–25, Mt 1:5, Heb 11:31), and Judith and Esther. And there are prophetesses, such as Miriam, the sister of Moses and Aaron (Ex 15: 20–21), and Deborah (Jgs 4:4–14, 5:1–31) and Huldah (2 Kgs 22:14–20). These women, however, are exceptions. The Jewish woman is primarily the guardian of the home and the mother of her children. She does not become involved in business or religion.

Jesus begins a new promotion of women. His condemnation of divorce implies an equality of duties between men and women, whereas Jewish law and customs were quite severe toward the unfaithful wife and much more tolerant toward the husband. Only the husband was able to "repudiate," and he was accused of adultery only if he had had an affair with a married woman. (See Mt 5:27–28, 31–32, 19:9. Compare these New Testament texts with Lv 5:11–31 and Dt 22:22, 24:1–4.)

Contrary to every custom, Jesus speaks freely with a woman (Jn 4:27) and shows indulgence toward a notoriously sinful woman (Lk 7:36–50) and the woman who was caught in a flagrant act of adultery (Jn 8:1–11). He enjoys being the house guest of his two friends, Mary and Martha (Lk 10:38–42), and associates a group of women in his ministry (Lk 8:1–3). Women are found near the cross (Lk 23:49) and at the tomb. Also, women are given the responsibility of announcing to the eleven the Resurrection of Jesus (Mt 28:8–10, Lk 24:9–11, Jn 20:17–18).

The image of the *perfect* woman is fully realized in the person of Mary, wife and virgin, mother and widow. That is surely the profound reason why Jesus solemnly calls her "Woman" (Jn 2:4, 19:26). She has dignity not only from the fact that she is "the Mother of the Lord" (Lk 1:43) —that privilege depended on God's free choice— she is "blessed among all women" because she "believed in the fulfillment of the words that were spoken to her by the Lord" (Lk 1:42–45) and because she heard God's word and kept it (Lk 11:28). Also, she became the "mother" of the disciple whom Jesus loved, the disciple who represented the entire Church, founded on charity (Jn 19:26–27).

8. THE NEW COVENANT OF THE PEOPLE OF GOD
(Jer 31:31–32a, 33–34a)

As we will say in the text that we suggest for the homily, we might ask ourselves how this pericope from Jeremiah can be related to marriage. Indeed, the brief passage (which is complete only with verse 34, which was omitted in our first reading) is Jeremiah's "highest peak of spirituality" (the Jerusalem Bible's notation on vv. 31–34). Even more must be said. Jer 31:31–34 is the most important of all revealed texts.

Because Jeremiah was announcing "the new covenant," is is not surprising that we find numerous echoes of the passage in the New Testament. It is cited and commented on in Heb 8:6–13 and 10:15–18. It is the underlying text in the Discourse on the Bread of Life (Jn 6:45 quotes a closely related passage from Is 54:13) and also in many of St. Paul's passages on "internal" law, the law of the Spirit (Rom 8:2–4, 2 Cor 3:3, etc.). Moreover, Jesus himself refers to this text when he institutes the Eucharist (Lk 22:20, 1 Cor 11:25, and all the Eucharistic prayers).

Because we are gathered for the joy-filled ceremony of marriage, it may seem surprising to hear a reading from the prophet Jeremiah. Particularly for those who have never read him, the name of Jeremiah evokes sadness and lamentations. Nevertheless, although Jeremiah shared intensely in the trials and tribulations of his defeated and exiled people, he was also a great announcer of hope. The "Book of Consolation," the section of Jeremiah from which today's reading was taken, is well named because of the hope it offered to the Israelites.

The passage is not directly related to marriage; and yet Jeremiah is talking about marriage. You must have noticed that the word "covenant" was repeated three times. In today's language, "covenant" especially designates the rings that are worn by a married couple as a sign of their union, the rings that I will bless in a few moments.

Why does the ancient prophet speak of *covenant?* For Jeremiah, the word signifies the terms of the union God established with his people on Sinai when he gave them his law, the Ten Commandments: *The covenant I made with their fathers the day I took them by the hand to lead them forth from the land of Egypt.*

The union between God and his people is therefore presented to us as a marriage. The entire Bible speaks in the same manner. From cover to cover we encounter the image of the nuptial union between God and his people, between Christ and the Church, between God and humanity. In the Bible, "covenant" helps us understand how the marriage between a man and a woman is a great mystery, for marriage represents what is utmost in God's plan: that God be closely united to mankind in order to establish with us the most durable and most profound intimacy that can exist.

But in this passage Jeremiah does not remain a prisoner of the past. He looks toward the future by announcing a *new covenant*. The main foundation of the old covenant was law, the "external" commandments that were imposed on the will of the contracting parties.

The *new covenant* also contains legal duties and obligations; but the new law is no longer external, it is imposed from within. *I will place my law within them,* says God; *I will write it upon their hearts.* This is a living law, written in the very depths of our being by the Holy Spirit, in whom we have been baptized, the spirit of God whom we also call love.

At the moment when Jesus gave his disciples the greatest example of love by loving them "to the end" (Jn 13:1), he left them the sacrament of unity. He shared with them the bread that is his body and gave them to drink from the cup of wine that had become his blood, poured out for them. Then he said: "This is the cup of my blood, the blood of the new and everlasting covenant. It will be poured out for you." Now that the faithful can literally obey Christ's commandment, "Take and drink, all of you," it is especially fitting that the bride and groom on the day of their marriage drink of the same cup of the *new covenant.*

Our passage ends with a phrase that perhaps was not very surprising: *I will be their God, and they shall be my people.* This expression is like the motto of the covenant. In very simple terms it expresses the relationship and intimacy involved in such mutual sharing. The phrase is often repeated by the prophets, and it appears again at the end of the Bible in the book of Revelation (21:3), where the New Jerusalem, "beautiful as a bride prepared to meet her husband . . . comes down from heaven . . . to be God's dwelling among men." In the experience of eternal joy, "there shall be no more death or mourning, crying out or pain."

We can be certain that the phrase *I will be their God, and they shall be my people* is an expression of love, because the Song of Songs, in a passage that can also be read for the celebration of a marriage, repeats the same refrain when the bride cries out: "My lover belongs to me and I to him!" (Song 2:16, Old Testament reading 6).

NEW TESTAMENT READINGS

1. WHO WOULD BE ABLE TO SEPARATE US FROM CHRIST'S LOVE?
(Rom 8:31-35, 37-39)

A marriage is a wager on happiness! And St. Paul, in his Letter to the Romans, of which we have just heard a short passage, assures us that the wager will be won. But that doesn't mean that Paul is deceived by false optimism. The opening chapters of the same Letter to the Romans outline a very somber picture of the misery in which sin has plunged humanity (1:18–3:20). Then Paul immediately shows us how we win our freedom through faith, which unites us to Jesus Christ (3:21–7:25).

Finally, in chapter 8, the Apostle affirms that we are fully liberated by God's spirit, who is a Spirit of love. He makes that bold statement, which is not a part of our reading but which gives us the key to the entire passage: "We know that God makes all things work together for the good of those [who love God because they] have been called according to his decree" (8:28).

Isn't this an illusion or a Utopia? Can we ignore everything that troubles us? Does Paul mean that in your lifetime you will not encounter dangers, contradictions, failures, grief? No, he does not ignore any of these problems. He enumerates at length, especially in two passages (8:35 and 8:38–39), all that can obstruct our happiness. But he adds, with certainty, that we will always be able to overcome these difficulties.

How does Paul arrive at such certitude? From one fact: *God is for us,* because *he did not spare his only Son,*[1]

1. All the translations that we were able to consult read as follows: "He did not spare his only Son." It is true that in Paul, $\phi\varepsilon i\delta o\mu\alpha i$, the verb that is used in this passage, generally has the meaning of managing, economizing, sparing. But current English usage of "did not spare" connotes cruel and overpowering treatment. This cannot fit the meaning of our passage. On the other hand, the same verb is used in the Greek Bible in Gn 22:12, which everyone translates as "You did not withhold [refuse] your own beloved Son." Moreover, there is a strong indication that in this passage Paul is referring to the sacrifice of Isaac. "Not to refuse" is equivalent to the analogous word "'giving," which we cited in Jn 3:16.

but handed him over for the sake of us all. St. John says the same thing in 3:16: "God so loved the world that he gave his only Son."

Contrary to what is often stated, Christianity is not a religion of sadness, it is a religion of happiness and love. Of course, we cannot deny that pain exists and that human life is filled with failures, hardships, and injustices—and that the most intolerable situation is to witness the suffering of the innocent. Christianity does not deny any of this. On the contrary, at the very heart of the Christian mystery is the suffering of the innocent, the suffering of Jesus Christ, the holy one *par excellence.*

The suffering and death of God's Son, however, are transformed into liberation and joy by his Resurrection. And because the Son of God is our brother and leader by reason of his humanity, we too can transform our suffering and trials into victory, liberation, and ultimately joy.

Through baptism we died with Jesus Christ and have been raised with him. When two baptized people marry, they intensify their imitation of Christ and are more closely united to him in his death and Resurrection. Their marital love reflects and incarnates both the love that they have for God and the love that God has for them: "We know that God makes all things work together . . . according to his decree." And can we not believe today, with a sure faith, that this marriage of two Christians was foreseen in God's plan of love, *according to his decree?*

By offering Christ in the Mass and by offering yourselves with him, you show that you accept Christ as the person who witnesses and authorizes your union. Furthermore, by communicating in the body and blood of the risen Lord you share in his victory over evil. *Yet in all this you are more than conquerors. . . . Nothing will be able to separate you from the love of God that comes to us in Christ Jesus, our Lord.*

Nothing will be able to separate you from each other. Nothing will be able to divide your love.

2. THE NEW LIFE OF CHRISTIANS
(Rom 12:1-2, 9-18 [Long Form], 12:1-2, 9-13 [Short Form])

With the long and short forms of reading 2, the lectionary gives us just about the same text. The only difference is the suppression of verses 11-13 in the shorter form. Quantitatively, the elimination of a few verses is negligible, but qualitatively—in rendering the full meaning—the elimination of verse 13 is regrettable. Verse 13 deals with hospitality, which is a major duty of Christians in general and of the Christian home in particular. In our commentary, we suggest one homily for these two closely related passages. We have placed within parentheses whatever corresponds to the three verses that are omitted in the short form.

St. Paul's exhortation, which we have just heard, is addressed to all believers. Nevertheless, when it is proclaimed, as it is today, in the context of marriage, we sense that the passage takes on a very special flavor, because it is then applied to the Christian home. You recall from the passage all the words that fit the home situation: tenderness, holiness, love, affection, respect (generosity, hope, joy, perseverance, sharing, hospitality), agreement, simplicity, peace.

Indeed, this sounds like a litany of all the qualities that shoud be hoped for in your union. There is so much that I would be unable to give a detailed description of all these virtues. But you have your entire lifetime to meditate on this beautiful ideal and to achieve it.

First of all, I must calm your fears by giving you the real meaning of the first sentence: *I beg you through the mercy of God, to offer your bodies as a living sacrifice.* That does not mean that you have to sacrifice yourselves in the sense of immolating yourselves, of suffering. Unfortunately, in the current use of our language the word "sacrifice" has taken on this sad, negative meaning; it evokes destruction and privation. Actually, that is the opposite of the real meaning of sacrifice.

In the religious sense of the word, "sacrifice" evokes consecration to God, communion with God, and consequently enrichment. Therefore, because you want to have your marriage celebrated in church, before the altar and in the context of the Mass, you have come to *offer your bodies*—your two bodies—*as a living sacrifice.* Your two lives will henceforth be but one life, *holy and acceptable to God.*

And yet there are demands that will be made on you. That is what Tobiah meant when he said to Sarah on their wedding night, in a beautiful Old Testament passage: "We cannot unite ourselves like pagans who do not know God." Paul tells you the same thing: *Do not conform yourselves to this age,* which seeks in marriage only pleasure and "self-fulfillment" and sees nothing that is holy, generous, or definitive. Paul goes on to say: *Be transformed by the renewal of your mind, so that you may judge what is God's will.*

What is the will of God? *Your love must be sincere,* which means without pretense or falsity. Paul's exhortation may seem insulting to you; but it does not mean that there is pretense in your love. Instead, the passage puts you on guard against the false appearances of love. Indeed, even the most passionate love can be a form of selfishness, which is a far cry from true charity. Selfishness closes us in ourselves and does not allow us to be open to others. God's love, which is complete openness, must be the model of human love.

Love one another with the affection of brothers. Your reciprocal love can be of such a unique quality as to make you one in being. But your love should not cut you off from your brothers and sisters. You must not consider that the people who live and exist outside of your relationship form only, as it were, a backdrop for your love, or that the only purpose of humanity is to furnish you with agreeable or useful relationships. *Anticipate each other in showing respect.* That means that you should regard others as children of God, as persons who have divine worth.

(Your home must also be charitable. Love and charity are synonymous, at least with regard to the genuine love expressed in *generosity.* True love consists not merely in good words but in deeds of *sharing*: the sharing of devotion and service. Why shouldn't there also be a sharing of material things?

(*Be generous in offering hospitality* means that your home must be open to others. In the Christian home, hospitality is a duty, even when a family has only modest means. A home is open to others not only in its rooms and at its table but also, and especially, in the welcome and in the smile of those who live there. Paul asks Christians to be willing to open their hearts whenever they open their door.)

Your charity will be shown by the way you welcome even people who are disagreeable and hostile: *Bless your persecutors; bless and do not curse them.* Your welcome is not to be vague and passive. It will be so sympathetic that you will have an active and cordial interest in the joys and pains of the other person. A very beautiful thought is contained in the admonition *Rejoice with those who rejoice, weep with those who weep.*

People who act in this manner resemble that first community whose fervent Christian charity is described in the Acts of the Apostles: "The community of believers were of one heart and one mind" (Acts 4:32). We can also admire the way in which the early Christians lived, with "exultant and sincere hearts" (Acts 2:46). Paul in turn makes this recommendation to you: *Do not be wise in your own estimation.* That is one of the conditions of joy, a condition that will enable you to *live peacefully with everyone.*

Here, then, is the magnificent program of radiant perfection that Paul, in the name of love, proposes to all

believers in Christ. May Christ himself bless your love
and grant that you will realize this ideal.

3. "YOUR BODY IS A TEMPLE OF THE SPIRIT" (1 Cor 6:13c–15a, 17–20)

This text is especially difficult, and we risk having
it misunderstood or even judged unintelligible by listeners, who contrast body and soul, just as they distinguish
matter and spirit.

The passage has meaning only if, according to anthro-
pology and biblical language, the word "body" designates
the entire human being in his eternal destiny.[2] In our
suggested homily, we attempt to elucidate the biblical concept of body.

It seems to us that the value of this interpretation is
supported by the coherence it gives to the whole text and,
in particular, to a phrase that has been appropriately omitted in the liturgical text. The phrase, however, is important if we are to understand St. Paul's thought in verse
13a and b: *Food is for the stomach, and the stomach for
food, and God will do away with them both in the end.*

If by "body" we understand the material part of man,
we might ask: Why shouldn't God destroy such things as
the stomach and food? They correspond to a particular
function that is necessary for existence here on earth, and
it is understandable that these things will disappear when
death occurs. If, however, we take "body" to mean man in
his entirety, man as a complete entity, redeemed by the
suffering to which Christ submitted in the flesh when he
placed his spirit in the hands of his Father, that body is
indeed destined for resurrection and everlasting life. Finally, we also know that Paul said: *The body is for the
Lord, and the Lord is for the body.*

---

2. See the article "Body" in X. Leon-Dufour's *Dictionary of Biblical
Theology* (rev. ed.; New York, 1973).

Because it is difficult to comment on the text in a homily before a mixed gathering, it seems important that we read and explain it to the engaged couple while they are preparing for marriage. Although the text does not directly pertain to the doctrine of marriage, it reveals an essential principle, often ignored, that is a foundation for marriage, namely, the dignity of the body.

Perhaps the first reading, which we have just heard, was a shock to you. The word "body," is mentioned seven times! Wouldn't we expect the Church to be somewhat more spiritual and more idealistic? But that is precisely the serious misconception that some people have about the Christian faith. Our religion is not a sublime spiritualism that regards the body as a "rag"[3] and man as "a fallen god who remembers heaven."[4]

Christianity is the religion of the Incarnation, in which the Word became flesh in order to come and dwell among us. It is the religion of redemption, in which our Savior redeems us by suffering, dying, and rising for us in his body. The flesh therefore plays an important role in the plan of salvation, which is established by God.

And so it is not surprising that there is a sacrament, marriage, that is designed to recognize and sanctify love. That does not mean, however, that marriage dissolves love into a sublime unreality.

Christianity's rejection of idealism, nevertheless, does not cause us to fall into negative materialism. This is indeed the risk we take if we follow many Western philosophies and ideologies that continue to consider man as constituted by two opposite substances: matter and spirit.

---

3. It was A. Philaminte who gave the body such a contemptuous label. Chrysale's reply agrees with the biblical concept of body: "Yes, *my body is me,* and I wish to take care of it. 'However destitute, number one is dear to me!'" (*Les Femmes savants,* Act II, scene 1).

4. The quote is from Lamartine, who, as we know, was a very vague sort of Christian.

For the Bible, and therefore for St. Paul, whom we have just heard, body and soul are not opposing forces. "Body" designates man, considered in his totality as a living, visible creature, who takes his place in the world of creatures. Man's body is the center of his relationships with his brothers and sisters, because people cannot communicate with each other except through that intermediary, that sign which is the human body.

Jesus Christ did not come "to save souls." That kind of expression is nowhere found in the New Testament. Jesus came to save people, and therefore to save bodies. He was raised from the dead. But this doesn't mean that he became a "spirit," a phantom (see Lk 24:39). He was raised in his body. And because our humanity is linked to his, *God who raised the Lord, will raise us also by his power* (see 1 Cor 15:12, 20–22).

We were first united to Christ through our baptism. That is what Paul teaches us and what the Church recalls at each Easter Vigil in the Epistle of the Mass: *Do you not see that your bodies are members of Christ?* Therefore we should respect our bodies, which are consecrated in holiness and destined for eternal life.

Yes, the Christian must avoid impurity. Such avoidance, however, does not flow from hatred for the body, or from fear of being contaminated from the outside, as if some kind of taboo were violated. Even in marriage, which permits carnal union and sanctifies it with the pleasure that man and woman can take from their union, the husband and wife must shun impurity, because their union is both the effect and the sign of their deep love. *Every other sin a man commits is outside his body.* That is, such sins are more or less an accident, something external to his person. *But the fornicator sins against his own body,* in the sense that impurity touches not only his flesh but his deepest being, his relationships with himself, with his neighbor, and with God.

Paul goes even further and adds another trait to what we can call his eulogy of the body. He often uses the expression "you must know" to emphasize an important teaching that he often had to repeat. In this passage, the teaching is that *your body is a temple of the Holy Spirit.* Just as Jesus once compared his body to the Temple in Jerusalem (Jn 2:19–22), our bodies are consecrated to God by baptism, by the Eucharist, by the sanctity of marriage, and by prayer (see 1 Cor 3:16–17, 6:9, 2 Cor 6:16).

Therefore Paul's conclusion is not: Despise your body, forget your body, escape from your body. He says: With your entire life, which is physical, spiritual, and social— not along with or despite marriage but thanks to marriage— *glorify God in your body!*

4. A EULOGY ON GENUINE LOVE
(1 Cor 12:31–13:8a)

We have heard one of the most famous sections of St. Paul, his eulogy of genuine love, or, if you prefer, his eulogy of genuine charity. Charity does not really mean almsgiving and a condescending pity toward the poor but rather God's love, alive in us and reaching our brothers and sisters through us. Paul's eulogy of love is addressed to all Christians, but it applies in a special way to marriage, the sacrament of love, that excellent form of charity that is conjugal love.

Paul begins by placing us on guard against heroic exploits and extraordinary feats that, if they lack genuine love, are absolutely stripped of value. Don't we find heroic exploits and extraordinary feats in the romantic, foolish, exclusive, and egotistical love that popular novels, plays, and songs constantly invite us to admire as the only "genuine" kind of love? This does not mean that genuine love ought to be wearisome and mediocre; but going to unwarranted extremes and "breaking records" always risks nourishing our vanity and tempts us to use life without making essential demands on ourselves.

In marriage we are dealing with a love that must continue all through life, and it's very natural that its beginnings are particularly enrapturing and passionate. But if such a beginning is not sustained by genuine charity, there is a danger that it will not last. It will quickly burn itself out and disappear in the boredom of routine and acceptance of mediocrity. Paul wants us to understand that love is meant to endure and that, far from fading through contact with the realities of everyday life, love must become strong, grow deeper, and blossom more and more as each day passes.

Paul's entire teaching, as we learn from his other letters, obliges us to acknowledge that genuine love has a divine, supernatural source. Inasmuch as love flows from God's love and Christ's love, the love that is realized in us is a demanding love (2 Cor 5:14). After placing us on guard against the spectacular counterfeits of love, he embarks on a sort of litany in which the activities and applications of love seem very ordinary. We can comment on the passage with two lines from Verlaine:

The life that is humble in its tedious and easy tasks
is a chore chosen with a longing for much love.[5]

We would be mistaken if we regarded Paul's words as an invitation to achieve the golden mean. When we give separate consideration to each manifestation of love as enumerated by Paul, they can seem quite dull and ordinary. But to realize all of them at the same time and in a consistent manner, we have to be animated with a love that is uniquely deep, ardent, and courageous.

Because it would take too long to comment on these loving manifestations one by one, I will select only those that seem to me to have a special value for the life of a married couple.

Love is patient. Patience can seem obvious—or rather useless—in love's early days, when each person finds the other perfect and "adorable." Nevertheless, in everyday

5. Paul Verlaine, *Sagesse*, VIII.

life, even in the life of people who love each other intensely, patience is indispensable. Despite the fact that we say two persons become one in the mystery of marriage, husband and wife nevertheless remain two, dissimilar persons. A man does not react like a woman, and that's good; two people can be complementary only if they are different. We should also mention the differences that stem from the diversity of sensitivity, upbringing, and family traditions. Without patience, love cannot endure. Patience must also be active and effective.

Love is kind. God gave woman to man so that she would be "a partner suitable to him" (Gn 2:18, Old Testament reading 2). But man must also be a "suitable partner" for his wife. Love can continue only when there is cooperation and mutual support.

Love is not jealous, because jealousy is a sign of selfishness. And so it follows that *love does not seek its own interest.* Here we touch upon an essential characteristic of genuine love: love is unselfish and seeks only the interests of the other person. Love gives, and does not attempt to possess the other person. Here, as elsewhere, we find the model of authentic love in Jesus. Paul says it precisely: "We must not be selfish. . . . Christ did not please himself" (Rom. 15:1, 3).

If genuine love is unselfish, it can only be peaceful and ready to forgive. *Love is not prone to anger; neither does it brood over injuries.* Paul then adds a remark that is meaningful for all of us. In our desire to be right, we tend to rejoice over a *wrong* that allows us to win our point when we see our criticisms and condemnations confirmed: See! It's just as I said! Genuine love *does not rejoice in what is wrong. There is no limit to love's forbearance.*

Perhaps these two sentences could be better translated as "Love excuses everything. Love has confidence in everything."

The essential quality of human love is much more positive than the patience that we considered just a moment ago. Confidence is one of the traits of genuine love, which is also friendship. Confidence destroys the roots of jealousy.

Our text ends with a short phrase that has considerable importance: *Love never fails.* The continuing quality of love can be like a climax of everything that went before. Yes, if love is patient, kind, unselfish, and trusting, it must endure. In a way, a proof for this is given within our text: A love that is exempt of all that divides, all that embitters, all that closes one in on oneself, is a genuine love that has placed at a distance everything that is harmful to love, everything that could corrode love from within.

Love never fails has yet another meaning from the fact that the phrase is not merely the conclusion of what preceded it. Paul's text continues beyond what you have heard and moves toward perspectives of fulfillment and eternity: "When the perfect comes . . . when I shall know God even as he knows me" (vv. 10, 12), then many earthly realities will disappear. These realities are precious and even indispensable here below, but they have nothing at all to do with the fullness of perfection in eternal happiness. Only love will continue to be precious and indispensable, because the love of God and the love of others, including fraternal love and conjugal love, are of the same nature and have the same guarantees of perfection and eternity.

Heaven is love. Heaven is charity. We will go to heaven only if, at the end of our earthly life, we are found to be in love, in charity. Charity will not disappear. Our ties of charity will continue to exist in heaven. In this sense, it is true that Christian spouses are "companions for eternity."[6]

That is the life you are about to begin in being united to each other through the bonds of Christian marriage, through the bonds of a love that comes from God. Frail

6. See A. M. Carré's book with the same title (London, 1947).

creatures though we are, we love with a love that longs for eternity. From this moment on, you are entering eternity.

5. THE MYSTERY OF MARRIAGE
(Eph 5:2a, 21–33 [Long Form], 5:2a, 25–32 [Short Form])

If the shorter form, which omits verses 21–24, is the reading selected, the section of our commentary within parentheses may be disregarded. The short form also omits verse 33, but since the verse is merely the summary of the whole passage, we do not refer to it in the commentary.

The most beautiful passage on marriage in the entire New Testament is found in St. Paul's letter to the Ephesians, from which you have heard a section in the first reading.

The whole Letter to the Ephesians develops the theme of unity with genuine enthusiasm. The letter deals with the unity of all Christians among themselves—unity with Christ through baptism, faith, and love. Christians are united together to form the Church that Paul calls the body of Christ, and also the spouse of Christ. Therefore it was inevitable that Paul would give some consideration to marriage, because marriage is the sacrament of love and unity. The grace of Christian marriage flows from the grace of baptism, and through marriage the spouses form one body.

The mystery of marriage is derived from Christ, who is the model of unselfish and self-giving love. The remainder of our commentary relies on the fundamental principle: *Follow* [literally, "walk, advance, make progress in"] *the way of love even as Christ loved you. He gave himself for us.*

(Nevertheless, this epistle, which for centuries was the required Epistle in the wedding Mass, is looked down

upon by young women, because the passage instructs them
to be submissive to their husbands. That, they claim, is
a very outdated attitude!

(It is true that in the old Roman Missal our epistle
began in an almost brutal manner, with provocative in-
junction: *Wives should be submissive to their husband as
if to the Lord.* The phrase perhaps corresponded to a
particular concept of marriage, but in any case it distorted
Paul's thought. Not only was there omission of a command
addressed to everyone to imitate Christ by living a life of
love, there was omission of that primary rule, which is
applicable to all: *Defer to one another.*

(The deferring or submission demanded by Paul does
not have a one-sided meaning; it is reciprocal. For example, Paul says in another letter: "Out of love, place yourselves at one another's service" (Gal 5:13). If wives must
be submissive to their husbands, their submission is only
a particular application of a general law that is imposed
on all Christians. I realize that Paul adds *as if to the Lord,*
because *the husband is head of his wife just as Christ is
head of the Church*; but in place of "head" we might give
a better translation by the word "leader." And we know
in what manner Christ is our head and leader: *He loved
us; he gave himself up for us.* He is our Savior by becoming our slave. That is what Jesus said about himself: "The
Son of Man has come not to be served by others, but to
serve" (Mt 20:28). He took "the form of a slave . . .
obediently accepting even death" (Phil 2:7, 8).

(If we read the Epistle to the Ephesians without prejudice, we must recognize that it also makes special demands on the man, the husband.)

Therefore the husband's love for his wife must imitate
Christ's love for the Church. It may seem strange to us to
compare the Church to a wife, but that's because the word
"Church" reminds us of either a building or an authori-
tarian structure. The Church, however, is made up of the
people of God, people who are recruited throughout the
world, and especially the people who were first chosen by
God, the people of Israel.

In the Bible, the relationships between God and his people are described as the result of a "covenant," a word that makes us think of marriage. That is why the prophets so often show us a God who treats his people as a wife, that is, with tenderness and trust. God also treats this figure with severity when she is unfaithful to him, but he shows limitless mercy when she returns to him. It was therefore quite natural that the Church, redeemed humanity, be compared to a wife.

And Christ is the husband: *He loved the Church. He gave himself up for her,* because he loved people to such an extent that he willingly died for them, offering himself in sacrifice for their salvation and their happiness.

Christ's love as husband is therefore an entirely unselfish, recklessly generous love. Christ loves without expecting anything in return.

Jesus went beyond merely saving his "wife." He wanted to *make her holy and immaculate, without stain or wrinkle or anything of that sort.* Isn't that always what a lover desires? Jesus, however, is not satisfied with just wishing her to be beautiful, and he created what is impossible for a human husband to create. He made her beauty and holiness a reality *in the bath of water by the power of the word.* Baptism, *the bath of water,* removes what remains of the first sin. God's *word,* which invites us to respond in faith, communicated Christ's very life to us, the life we call grace.

By reason of this unity of life, Paul often calls the Church the body of Christ. He calls her by that name in the beginning of the Letter to the Ephesians (1:23, see also Col 1:18). Later in the letter he says the same thing: "Make every effort to preserve the unity which has the Spirit as its origin. . . . There is but one body and one Spirit," who is God's spirit, the Holy Spirit, the Spirit of love. "There is one Lord, one faith, one baptism" (4:3–4).

And since, in citing Paul, I again make mention of baptism, it must be noted that your baptism is the source of your Christian marriage. Through baptism you are part of the body of Christ. Through marriage, two baptized people are made one being in Christ.

Paul then quotes the words that we read in the book of Genesis, at the conclusion of the narrative on the creation of woman: *A man . . . shall cling to his wife, and the two shall be made into one* (Gen 2:24, Old Testament reading 2 and Gospel readings 4 and 6).

Since we have made reference to Christ and the Church, the mystery of marriage is therefore *a great mystery,* a great sacrament. You are about to celebrate this sacrament with great respect and emotion as you unite yourselves to each other for life. And you will seal this union by offering yourselves together with Christ as you partake of the same bread that has become his body and as you drink from the cup of his blood, the sign and the guarantee of the new and everlasting covenant.

6. LIVING IN PEACE AND THANKSGIVING (Col 3:12-17)

The ceremony of marriage lasts but a few moments, but these moments are decisive because they involve a whole lifetime. Therefore, so that your life together will be happy, smooth, and harmonious, you must do what St. Paul told us in a passage from his Letter to the Colossians. He described the ideal of family life in this epistle in such a striking way that each year we read the same passage on the feast of the Holy Family of Jesus, Mary, and Joseph of Nazareth.[7]

Basically, all these counsels are summarized in one, which will not seem too difficult to understand: the coun-

---

7. To be more precise, Col. 3:12–21, which is four verses longer than our reading, is read. These four verses address wives, husbands, children, and parents in succession. Surely, the four verses are omitted in the marriage reading because the first two exhortations seem somewhat dull on a wedding day and the latter verses a little premature.

sel of love. But isn't there a question here of merely superficial sentiment, of passing, momentary excitement or
quaint sentimentality? On the contrary, this love is serious, solid, and enduring: *Clothe yourselves with heartfelt
mercy, with kindness.*

If you think that Paul's advice seems much too natural, he continues with something that is more austere and
difficult: *Clothe yourselves with heartfelt . . . humility,
meekness and patience.*

Permit me to speak to you in today's terminology:
The honeymoon will not last forever! Try as you may to
become one with each other, you will soon see that your
differences will reveal themselves once again: differences
of character, temperament, and especially that indescrib-
able difference that obtains between a man and a woman.
One of you will often be more outgoing, and the other
more concerned with the intimacy of the home. One may
be more concerned with material details, while the other
likes sentimental niceties. Either the man or the woman
will have a more expansive religious fervor, and the other
spouse a more austere religion. Because of family tradition, there will be differences in judgment on politics, the
way to deal with relatives, or the demands of hospitality.

Even husbands and wives who love each other deeply
can attach more or less importance—one a great deal and
the other not much at all—to a detail in life such as neat-
ness. There are many degrees or levels in the style of
family comfort, personal preference, and eating habits that
can place obstacles between two very loving people. From
these differences can come frequently recurring arguments.

You must therefore have a heart filled with *humility*
so as not to impose on your spouse your way of looking
at things. You must have a heart full of *meekness* so that
you will learn to laugh when you're about to take something too seriously. You must have a heart full of *patience*
to sustain all the little pains of everyday life, without turn-
ing them into tragedies.

Bear with one another; accept your inequalities; recognize your differences. You have to see that the life you

share cannot always be a song sung in unison, which would quickly bore you. There is far greater richness and, indeed, much more sweetness in a symphony that brings diverse but complementary parts together.

Paul goes even further. He calls our attention to real conflicts that can arise due to faults and failings. In such circumstances, he says, *forgive whatever grievances you have against one another.* And he shows the sublime model of genuine love, the decisive model for Christians: *Forgive as the Lord has forgiven you.* Isn't that what we commit ourselves to do each time we recite the Lord's Prayer?

Paul then gives us a magnificent but somewhat mysterious precept: *Over all these virtues put on love, which binds all the rest together and makes them perfect.*

Over all these virtues. Let us not picture love, however, as some sort of brilliant cover, designed to mask deep differences. Love is not a cloak that hides what a person is wearing. Rather, Paul describes love as a bond, a kind of belt or fastening that pulls together, in unity and perfection, all the different elements and all the centrifugal tendencies of two diverse personalities. Without a vibrant, active love that continues to bring husband and wife together in a profound unity, the couple would be menaced, day after day, with divisiveness and conflict.

And so, because love wins out in the end, there will be *peace.* This does not mean a fragile truce, or simply the absence of conflict. This peace is the kind that we must relentlessly build each day by conquering our self-love, our desire to dominate and "be right" in every situation. *Christ's peace must reign in your hearts, since as members of the one body you have been called to that peace.*

Paul concludes his exhortation with an appeal: *Dedicate yourselves to thanksgiving.* What does he mean? Earlier, he reminded you that you have been chosen by God and that you are his beloved people (verse 12). It is for happiness that he has chosen both of you—yes, the two of you—for each other. The love that unites you is only a reflection of the infinite love by which God loves you. Isn't that a magnificent blessing, an unmerited gift and privilege? You must therefore *sing gratefully to God from your hearts.*

There can be two very diverse attitudes when we consider God's love and human love. There is the jealous, egotistical attitude of the person who believes that he has everything coming to him. Such a person will never stop complaining. He—or she—feels cheated. They will never admit that they are loved enough or that someone else makes enough sacrifices for them. Such a love cannot endure. It induces a druken-like stupor and is self-destructive.

By contrast, there is the grateful, unselfish love that is always joyful and satisfied, because the persons believe that life owes them nothing. They see the love that they receive as absolutely undeserved, as an unbelievable, miraculous godsend! This love lasts, because it knows how to support and forgive.

Genuine love is not content with receiving and enjoying. It gives, because it finds much more joy in loving than in being loved. Such love is the image of the love of God, who loves us though he has no need for us.

I pray that the marriage we are celebrating will result in such a joy-filled and grateful love. That is what we pray for in the Mass, which is the setting for your marriage.

Paul concludes by saying: *Let the word of Christ, rich as it is, dwell in you.* The readings, which you heard a few moments ago, gave you a glance at some of that richness. Now, in offering the bread and wine of the Eucharist, you will fulfill Paul's command: *Do everything in the name of our Lord Jesus Christ. Give thanks to God the Father through him!*

7. THE UNION AND PEACE OF THE CHRISTIAN HOME
(1 Pt 3:1–9)

St. Peter insists: *You married women must obey your husbands.* Now the women who are here today should not be unduly disturbed by this command!

This scriptural passage is part of a development that begins with a recommendation that citizens be loyal toward civil authority, even if that authority is held by pagans (2:13–17). Slaves are told to obey their masters conscientiously, even if their masters are disagreeable and unjust (2:18–25). In all these difficult situations Peter invites Christians to imitate the humility of Jesus, who came not to be served but to serve. Therefore he insists that a wife be united to her husband, even if the man does not share her faith.

Such a situation happened frequently in the early Church, and it is not unusual today. Indeed, whenever this situation occurs, the wife should be able to be an apostle for her husband, not by making speeches that might cause him to stiffen his resistance but by the irresistible radiance of her *conduct,* by *the reverent purity of her way of life.* It is a general law that we are more influential by what we do, rather than by what we say. We are even more influential by what we essentially are as persons.

If the husband is a Christian, he will perhaps be much more appreciative of the purity and dignity that will prevail in his home.

In the same letter, Peter states that baptized people are called to be "a chosen race, a royal priesthood, a holy nation, a people God claims for his very own." Therefore if both husband and wife share in Christ's priesthood and holiness, won't the home that is created by their union in Christ be a sacred place?

Ladies, St. Peter warned you about flirtation. Although you may consider his warning severe and stilted, you should understand what he means. He calls attention to profound virtues that are far more important than a woman's adornment.[8] And yet he does not mean that external beauty has no importance or that it would be virtuous for a woman to make herself ugly or neglect herself. Our body is a creation of God and we have a duty of charity toward it. Love, a wife's charity toward her husband, obliges her to be attractive to him and lovable. This is an important factor in the charm and solidity of every home.

Peter then goes on to speak to men. He invites them to *show consideration* for women. And how difficult men find it to be considerate! *Treat women with respect as the weaker sex* does not mean that women are weak or inferior, although that is how women were considered in a social sense, in the time of St. Peter. What he asks of the Christian husband is not the protective and paternalistic condescension that is shown toward a minor.

The great novelty of Christianity—then as always—is remove or to minimize social and racial segregation. St. Paul puts it forcefully: "All of you who have been baptized into Christ have clothed yourselves with him. There does not exist among you slave or freeman, male or female. All are one in Christ Jesus" (Gal. 3:27–28). Peter says the same thing in a less direct manner, but in a way that is richer and more positive: Wives *are heirs just as much as you [husbands] to the gracious gift of life.*

In the community of the home, there must not only be equality but perfect spiritual communion. And if that happens, *nothing will keep your prayers from being answered.* In the sanctuary that is the Christian home, you must manifest your faith and love of God in family prayer.

8. According to every translation, it appears that Peter condemns flirtation: "Do not dress up for show" (Jerusalem Bible); "The donning of rich robes is not for you" (the New American Bible). The French lectionary adds the word "only," not so much to make the text more acceptable to our modern mentality but accurately to translate the familiar Semitic idiom that indicates a negative where we make a comparison.

But the love of God cannot develop freely unless love of neighbor—therefore conjugal love—prevails in your home.

If in your home life you are *like-minded,* you will be fully *sympathetic, loving toward one another, kindly disposed and humble.* Your life will be visible from the outside, which is precisely the significance of the word "home." A home is not just a married couple, or a family closed in on itself, but a center that is open and attractive. The friends whom each of you has should not be saddened by your marriage, as though marriage will remove you from their friendship! On the contrary, they ought to rejoice, because your union should pay dividends on the sympathy that each of you already possesses.

At this moment, as we celebrate your marriage, we wish that your union may call *a blessing* on others, and we pray that *you may receive a blessing as your inheritance.*

8. LOVING IN DEED AND IN TRUTH
   (1 Jn 3:18-24)

Christianity is a religion of love, and that is why there is a Christian sacrament of love, which is marriage. But we are not talking about a love of fantasy or a love in words alone. We mean a love that is lived out, a practical love, a love that is incarnated in everyday life.

A few moments ago St. John gave us an exhortation, or rather a command: *My little children, let us love in deed and in truth and not merely talk about it.* John spoke in that manner to the entire Christian community, because Jesus had said: "This is how all will know you for my disciples: your love for one another" (Jn 13:35).

It is necessary to bring the commandment of love to the attention of all Christians, who are often divided among themselves and oppose each other through jealousy, bitterness, social situations, and political choices. But does it serve any worthwhile purpose to give the commandment to people who are about to be married, who already love each other? Quite clearly, they are in love in a manner that is practical and *in truth*, because they are being married!

That is certain—at least for today. But what will happen in the future? Marriage is a ceremony of one day and one hour; yet marriage involves two people for a lifetime. And even though life may not bring great trials or great dramatic moments, life is exhausting, simply because it lasts a long time. By the very fact that we are creatures of habit, life has a way of making the most passionate and the most tender sentiments commonplace. Therefore down through the years love risks becoming a matter of words alone.

Although it is true that you are not forced to say "I love you" each and every morning of your lives, love tends to lose its simple memories and original spirit and to take on a tolerance or routine that no longer has any charm. And when that happens, the devitalized love may succumb to personality conflicts or financial problems. There may even be distractions, such as concern for the education of the children.

Today, you need to make an apparently simple resolution—a resolution that will nonetheless demand great concern and generosity on your part. The resolution calls for you to love each other not only for today but for tomorrow and beyond, *in deed and in truth*.

In deed—that is, with attentive care, anticipating the needs of the other person by positive acts, which means more than the absence of disagreeable actions or, alternatively, sheer passivity. Such positive deeds very often demand sacrifices, for whoever loves another person *in truth* loves that person for his or her own sake, not for oneself, or for one's own advantage, or for one's own satisfaction.

John's message leaves no doubt in our mind, because in his gospel he wrote Jesus' commandment to love in these explicit words: "Love one another as I have loved you" (Jn 15:12). Thus love should be generous and unselfish. Love should anticipate the needs of the other person.

To be more precise, Jesus loves us. By his love he helps us discover how God loves us, and he gave us his own love as an example. That is why John speaks to us about the Father: *His commandment is this: We are to believe in the name of his Son, Jesus Christ, and are to love one another as he commanded us.* The Father's commandment adds nothing new to the commandment of Jesus, who said: "Love one another as I have loved you."

Love, therefore, presupposes that we *believe in his Son, Jesus Christ.*

When we are young it often happens that we allow our faith in Jesus Christ to become obscure in our heart and mind. Later, marriage is frequently the occasion or, to be more exact, marriage frequently gives the grace to rekindle the light of our faith, because we understand that loving *in deed and in truth*—which is so necessary in a love that lasts a lifetime—means that we must love each other as Jesus has loved us. Therefore we trust in the love of God's Son toward men and obey his command as a command from God himself. In reality, that is what it means *to believe in his Son, Jesus Christ.*

Our being forgetful of Jesus, as well as the distance we sometimes place between Jesus and ourselves, can make us uneasy. But we must trust in the purification that comes to us in love that is like the love Jesus has for us, a love *in truth.* John says it in a striking manner: *This is our way of knowing that we are committed to the truth and are at peace before him . . . for God is greater than our hearts.* John means that even the most serious faults that we may have committed (and for which we are sorry) cannot discourage the mercy of God: his love is always ready to forgive.

That is why *we can be sure that God is with us and that we will receive at his hands whatever we ask . . . because . . . we are doing what is pleasing to him.*

You are about to be united before God. You have therefore decided to *keep his commandments,* the first of which is—and we shouldn't hesitate to repeat it—that we love one another as he has loved us. The prayers of all your friends accompany you. Their prayers should help sustain your confidence at this moment, as you commit yourselves to the great adventure of marriage.

9. GOD IS LOVE
(1 Jn 4:7–12)

God is love. You have heard St. John make this amazing statement, and he will repeat it later in his letter (4:8 and 4:16).

We are well aware that God is power, because believing in God means that we at least believe that he created the world. As do many philosophers, we also think of God as thought, intelligence, and knowledge of all things. Following many moralists, we believe that he is legislator, that he spells out what we must do and therefore that he knows and judges all our failures. But if we stop here, we run the risk of considering God not only as a morose personality but as someone who is stern and even dreadful, which is about the same as approaching God as a bogeyman. Thus it is easy to understand why many people seek to rid themselves of such a God, who would be the enemy of freedom and joy.

God is love! This is Christianity's most original and most daring affirmation. This statement makes Christianity a unique religion, as Paul Valéry, an unbeliever, recognized at the end of his life. St. John explains: *God's love was revealed in our midst in this way: he sent his only Son to the world that we might have life through him.*

Our belief in Jesus Christ means that we believe in a Savior, in God's Son, who has become our human brother. We also believe that *God is love.* God is not merely a good father who rewards his very bright children: *Love,*

*then, consists in this: not that we have loved God but that
he has loved us.* "He first loved us" (1 Jn 4:19).

Yes, John said it several times: *No one has ever seen
God, his Son has revealed him to us* (see Jn 1:18). To
receive this revelation, all we need do is read the gospels
or look upon a crucifix, because *God has loved us and has
sent his Son as an offering for our sins.*

But consider what we really do. We often pass before
the crucifix and no longer even notice it! We no longer
read in the gospels the quiet and yet eloquent revelation
of the God who is love. And even if we haven't completely
forgotten our catechism lessons, we regard this awesome
revelation as just one more item in a list of conventional
formulas.

Fortunately, John also tells us that God's love is revealed in the love that exists among people: *Love one
another, because love is of God.*

When we were little children, God's love was revealed
to us through the love our father and mother showed us
(because God is not only Father but Mother as well!).
Years later, as adults, we can experience the joy of being
loved and the joy of loving. We discover a creature who
loves us for ourself, someone who allows us to return love
in the same absolute manner. We do not love that person
as a useful thing or as a means to achieve our pleasure.
Here is a person like ourself, someone who comes to complete, enrich, and expand our life.

If we encounter genuine love in such a manner, we
truly receive a new revelation from God. From the very
fact that God is love, we know him not only by intelligence
alone, like a theory or a "dead" truth, we also know God
with our hearts, because he is a living truth. Because God
is interested in me, he regards me as though I were the
only person in the world.

Because *love is of God* and because *everyone who loves
is begotten of God,* the love between a man and a woman

can be a sacrament, the sacrament of marriage, which we have gathered together to celebrate.

Marital love can surely be mixed with many earthly realities, because we are human and are made of flesh and blood. But earthly realities are in no way to be condemned or even despised. They are somewhat similar to the "material aspect" of the sacraments, like water in baptism and like bread and wine in the Eucharist. A sacrament transforms its matter, and the transformation lasts for a lifetime.

Without the sacrament of marriage, *love,* which *is of God,* might slip into mutual selfishness or fade into a commonplace routine. But when the grace of the sacrament is sustained by daily devotion, which includes sacrifice, and by the constantly renewed gift of each person to the other, it will be possible, from day to day and from year to year, for love to grow and be purified and become deeper. Therefore an always new discovery of God will occur.

That will be our prayer of petition, especially in this Mass, because the Mass realizes the presence of that sacrifice and that meal in which God gives us his Son as *an offering for our sins.* God is clearly showing us that he has loved us first, and he gives us the opportunity to share in his love.

10. THE WEDDING FEAST OF THE LAMB OF GOD AND THE CHURCH
(Rv 19:1, 5–9a)

You have heard the reading of a passage from Revelation, which is also called the Apocalypse. Perhaps that word makes you uneasy because, in today's language, "apocalyptical" is synonymous with "terrifying" and "catastrophic." But in reality the Apocalypse is a book of encouragement and joy, especially in its final chapters, from which our reading is taken. The passage is particularly joyous because it transports us into *heaven*.

We do not conclude from the text that the state of marriage will thereby place you in heaven! Nevertheless, we must, as believers, every so often consider our final destiny, the happiness that God has promised us and toward which we are heading through all the trials of our earthly life.

Our text definitely deals with marriage and with a bride. The wife in question is the Lamb's spouse, the bride of Christ, Christ who is the Lamb of God who takes away the sin of the world. His bride is the Church. Even in the Old Testament, the covenant between God and his people was regarded as a marriage, which leads us to an important truth.

Not only are you being married "in church," you are being married in the Church. The home that you are starting thereby becomes a cell of the Church, a Church in miniature; and being a "little Church" means that married people should avoid being closed in on themselves in an egotism that is designed for only two people. Such selfishness makes people concentrate exclusively on their own salvation. As a married couple, you must also be concerned about the happiness and salvation of others. A married couple will experience genuine Christian happiness only by reaching out to the people around them.

In virtue of the magnificent dogma of the Communion of Saints, a married couple can influence even the entire world.

We should not be led to believe that the heavenly vision of the Apocalypse invites us to forget this life, or to escape into an unreal world where everything is easy. The greater part of the Apocalypse is an encouragement to Christians, who face the difficult struggle of life on earth. Heavenly visions, such as the one we have just heard, are not given to dispense us from the struggle and suffering of this life.

God's bride *has been given a dress to wear of fine linen, brilliant white,* because her wedding dress is sewn from *the virtuous deeds of God's saints,* sewn from their everyday lives of humility, effort, and perseverance. We are not being asked to escape from this life but rather to discover the splendor that even now is hidden in it. Therefore our reading is not an invitation to lose ourselves in a dream world, but a call to Christian realism.

In no way does realism imply dullness. The book of Revelation is an invitation to courage and hope. It is also a magnificent poetic fountain that reveals God's splendor and majesty, as well as his tenderness toward mankind. For this reason the Apocalypse is also an immediate invitation to prayer, especially the prayer of praise and thanksgiving.

The life of the Christian, in heaven and even now on earth, unfolds as a joyous and impressive liturgy, made up of processions in white vestments, with acclamations, with concerts of citharas and the aroma of perfumes.

In our reading, an angel has invited the heavenly inhabitants to a joy-filled thanksgiving. The invitation might also be given to people who live on earth, people who have confessed their belief in Christ and are aware that they are saved by baptism and grace. This invitation to praise can even more readily be given to husbands and wives who, through the sacrament of marriage, are perfecting their baptism and are growing in the grace of a holiness that they share in their relationship.

Praise our God, all you his servants, the small and the great, who revere him. And the crowd responds, as I hope you will also respond: *Alleluia! Let us rejoice and be glad, and give him glory! For this is the wedding of the lamb!*

Today we are celebrating an image and an effect of that heavenly wedding feast, in which you are sharing. But the two of you will continue this celebration every day of your life together.

By offering the Lamb at Mass, whose blood has taken

away the sin of the world, the two of you support the union, the joy, and the thanksgiving of the eternal wedding feast in heaven. At each Mass you will hear the priest invite you to communion, as will happen in a few minutes, when he repeats the words pronounced by the angel of the Apocalypse: *Happy are they who have been invited to the wedding feast of the Lamb!*

READINGS FROM THE
FOUR GOSPELS

1. THE BEATITUDES: THE PARADOX OF HAPPINESS ACCORDING TO THE GOSPEL (Mt 5:1–12a)

Despite the place St. Matthew gave it, the Sermon on the Mount cannot possibly have been Jesus' first sermon. It is intended for converts and believers, and proposes to them a complete catechesis on the Christian ideal. Therefore this gospel reading is not appropriate for the marriage of a couple who are hardly Christian. Especially, if it is not intended for the marriage of a couple who are not very serious about leading a life in conformity with the gospels.

On the other hand, it would be extreme to reserve the reading for an elite group of fervent believers. The "disciples" to whom Mt 5:1 refers are not entirely distinguishable from the "crowds" mentioned earlier. Also, the Second Vatican Council reminded us that all baptized Christians are called to perfection.

Because the gospel is not directly related to marriage, it would be appropriate to plan to have another reading that speaks explicitly of marriage, such as Old Testament readings 1, 2, and 3 (Gn), 4 and 5 (Tb), and New Testament readings 5 (Eph) and 7 (Pt).

A marriage is by definition a happy event! We are gathered here to wish this couple great and lasting happiness and to pray for their future happiness. We make this wish as we share in the joy they feel in their hearts.

Everyone desires happiness, and God wants happiness for everyone. It is an error, and I would go so far as to say it is a calamity, to present Christianity as a religion of mourning and sadness. The discourse or program that Matthew the Evangelist places on the lips of Jesus begins nine times with the word "blessed," which means happy!

And so these are wishes for happiness, pronounced by Jesus himself, which I extend to you today in his name.

But let us come out and say it: Jesus' wishes for

happiness are somewhat disconcerting!   Adapting another
quote of Jesus, we might hear him say: I wish you happiness, but it is not as the world wishes it for you. The world
wants happiness to go with riches, power, joy, pleasure, and
the satisfaction of every ambition. But I wish happiness
for you in poverty, meekness, tears, hunger and thirst for
justice, purity of heart, the building of peace, and even
persecution!

     To understand what Jesus means, let us look at the
First Beatitude, of which almost all the others are merely
consequences and applications.
     Blessed are the poor in spirit. Matthew, who certain-
ly followed Jesus' thought with great fidelity, specifies
that Jesus meant poverty *in spirit.* Material poverty, of
itself, is not a condition for happiness. Without even
going so far as to consider extreme misery, which is a
misfortune, it very often happens that the lack of material
comfort is accompanied by unrest, envy, and hatred. Such
extreme poverty does not bring the promise of happiness.
     On the other hand, people can have great material
wealth and still have poverty of spirit. Such people also
possess riches of another kind: *the reign of heaven is
theirs.* This means that they share in the very wealth and
happiness of God. Therefore the meaning of the expression *reign of heaven* is clear: God himself is the friend
and generous benefactor of impoverished hearts.
     What is meant by being poor in spirit? It means that
our hearts are not puffed up with pride and that we refuse
to trust in ourselves and in our riches, whether these
riches be material, cultural, or spiritual, trusting not even
in our ability to love. Having a "poor" heart means that
we recognize our essential poverty before God, who alone
is rich and from whom we expect to receive anything. A
"poor" heart is the heart of a child, who trusts with complete abandonment and simplicity.
     It is easy to understand how such a disposition en-
genders meekness, mercy, and purity.
     And how are we to understand *Blessed are the sor-*

rowing? First of all, in the sense that life, even the happiest life, is not a fairy tale. For each of us, life brings its share of trials, sufferings, and sadness. Whatever the perspectives of happiness in your home, sad experiences will not totally elude you.

Christianity, however, is not a religion of suffering. It takes things as they are and recognizes the part that suffering plays in life. Specifically, Christianity teaches us that suffering can not only be accepted with resignation, as an inevitable struggle, but that suffering should be accepted as a value that purifies and enriches us.

Of course, we do not seek suffering for its own sake. But if we willing accept suffering with the sentiments of a "poor" person, as a cross God offers to associate us with the cross of Christ, we will be *comforted.* This consolation will not be automatic and impersonal. God himself will console us if we learn not only to bear suffering but to offer it up with generosity.

There is another beatitude that I would like to stress: *Happy are those who hunger and thirst for what is right.*[1] We can be certain that in the Bible the idea of justice goes beyond the political and social connotations the word has in the language we use today. Biblical justice includes perfect "accuracy," which involves the accomplishment of our religious duties. In the Bible, justice also means "hitting the mark" perfectly in our relationships with other people: our superiors, our equals, our fellow workers, and also people who are most impoverished, most deprived, and most abandoned. Obviously, such justice includes charity. We must hunger and thirst for that kind of justice and consider it as essential to our life as bread and wine. As if by hunger and thirst, we are driven to fight for what is right whenever justice is violated and ridiculed in our world.

Now we come to the last of our beatitudes: persecu-

---

1. Translator's note: This translation is from the English Jerusalem Bible. The author states the beatitude as *Heureux ceux qui ont faim et soif de la justice* (Happy are those who hunger and thirst for justice.)

tion. "Persecution" seems to be a very important word, which we use when we want to describe a reality in a slightly melodramatic manner. Injustice is very widespread and, as it were, spontaneous. But justice so easily passes for Utopia and naive hope that people who hunger and thirst for it necessarily face contradiction and opposition, which can go so far as real persecution. Think, then, of Jesus, whose thirst for justice led him to the cross.

I will conclude my remarks with a less fearsome beatitude, which is more likely to blend with our hopes on a day like this: *Blessed too are the peacemakers.* However, such a translation leaves a little to be desired. It leads us to believe that happiness is promised to people who are lulled into meaningless tranquility and inertia. But the words of the gospel have a much stronger significance; they mean the artisans and builders of peace.

The word "peace" must be taken in its richest meaning, which it had in the words of Jesus' countrymen—and has even today in the language of children who greet you in Jerusalem with shouts of *Shalom!* "Peace!" This peace is not only tranquility and the absence of war. It is also harmony, health, prosperity, salvation for believers. All of these terms can be summarized in one word: happiness.

By being married, by giving yourselves to one another, by saying "yes" in the presence of Christ, you will accomplish an act of peace. You will also express your intention to construct peace in your home. Throughout your long life together, may your home breathe peace, and spread peace to those around it, especially to people who are often hostile toward one another and are torn apart in strife.

If peace will emanate from your home in this way, you will be *called sons* and daughters *of God.* Indeed, that's what you will be, because you will bear the resemblance of him who is your Father, the God of peace and happiness.

2. SALT OF THE EARTH AND LIGHT OF THE WORLD
(Mt 5:13–16)

This passage follows immediately after the beatitudes. Its teaching seems less paradoxical and less demanding, and so it could be used in a setting of less evangelical fervor.

For a long time the liturgy has used, and still uses, almost the same passage from St. Matthew for the feasts of Church Doctors, who are indeed in a very particular sense, the salt of the earth and the light of the world. But this liturgical choice could have been influenced mainly by verses 17–19, which are based on the teaching of the Jewish Law. These three verses are not retained in our reading. In any case, the short parables of salt and light, with the invitation to give good example, apply to all Christians.

Surely, marriage is not in question in the two parables, but the images of salt and light are taken from the daily life of the home. Salt is needed for food and, each evening, a light is turned on in the home.

The main point of the parables is that good example, which every Christian must radiate to the world, can be appropriately applied to the home life that the husband and wife are about to begin.

Salt belongs in the kitchen and it also serves to preserve food. Salt therefore has the meaning of stability and permanence. In the language of the Old Testament we read of a "covenant of salt," which signifies an indissoluble covenant (Nm 18:19). That is why salt was always used in the sacrifices that renewed the covenant (see Lv 2:13, Mk 9:49).

We can consider salt in still another way. Salt brings out the taste of food and makes it more appealing at the family table. Furthermore, through all antiquity salt was the symbol of hospitality. Even today it is a custom in certain countries to offer visitors "bread and salt" as a sign of hospitality.

Perhaps you were surprised to hear that salt can lose so much of its flavor and power that one would have to use salt on the salt itself. The salt that we use today does not "go flat," but in Judea the people often used slabs from the Dead Sea or salty lakes that were mixed with gravel and sand, which eventually crumbled. Clearly, such slabs no longer deserved the name of salt. Because the salt was useless in this form, it had to be thrown away.

With the parable of the lamp we find ourselves in the "visiting room." In Jewish homes at the time of Jesus, the visiting or hospitality room comprised the whole house and the kitchen was part of this room.

The lamp is like the symbol of a house that is lived in. For instance, when someone is lost in the country at night he is happy to see a light shining from afar in a window. The light fills this person with joy and attracts him to the house. The lamp, moreover, is not extinguished as long as the family continues to live in the house.

God promised David that he would always have a lamp at Jerusalem, which meant, according to the expression of the time (1 Kgs 11:36, 15:4, Ps 131 [132]:17), that his descendents "would not be extinguished." On the other hand, a snuffed-out lamp was the symbol of death (Jb 18:5–6, Jer 25:10).

Jesus tells us that it would be a strange thing to do to hide such a lamp under a basket. Quite clearly, the lamp is lit not only to give light but also to give *light to all in the house.* Therefore the lamp gives off not only brightness but joy.

As we know with our modern fixtures, a light that is soft and bright contributes to the pleasantness of a home. Indeed, light gives the impression of comfort, friendship, and peace, which visitors in that home share with the members of the family.

The significance of salt and a lamp in Palestine at the time of Jesus has not changed very much. But what is the moral application of the parables?

With regard to salt, we have seen that it signifies continuity by preserving food and by being used in the sacrifices that conclude a "covenant of salt," that is, an indissoluble covenant. Salt also signifies hospitality.

Therefore, on the occasion of this short parable, I wish that your union will be truly indissoluble, just as you wish it to be. I wish, too, that there will be a warm welcome and cordial hospitality in the joyful and peaceful atmosphere of your home, which is symbolized by the lamp.

But it seems to me that we can find another, more fundamental and more demanding significance in salt. What characterizes salt, as I see it, is that it has a taste of its own, a special savor that distinguishes it and allows a dash or two to highlight or bring out the taste of all foods.

Regardless of how numerous Christians are in the world, they must be *the salt of the earth*. By another gospel comparison, Christians must be the bit of yeast that makes the mass of dough rise. Christians must give an example of faithfulness and stability. But their obedience to the law of love cannot be followed without difficulties or contradiction from a crowd of people who want to live in "complete freedom." Christians must face temptations that arise from this world and from the complicity that we sometimes find within ourselves. People who wish to be real Christians should therefore be prepared to "renounce" themselves and make sacrifices.

There will always be differences among people and types of people. But their differences makes Christians worthwhile and, in the long run, win them the esteem of others. A Christian, or perhaps I should say the members of a Christian home, from time to time should ask an important question: If I were not a Christian, would I behave in the way I do? Does being a Christian make any impact on my life if I "act like everyone else"? What value is there in salt that has lost its savor, salt that is no longer salt?

The parable of the lamp is more appealing. Our Lord himself indicates that its meaning is the giving of good example: *Your light must shine before men so that they may see goodness in your acts and give praise to your heavenly Father.*

Some people object to this passage, along with other passages from the Sermon on the Mount, in which our Lord asks us not to give alms and not to fast and pray so as to be seen by others (Mt 6:1, 2, 5, 16). But there is no contradiction here, and comparison of a lamp with *a city set on a hill* helps us to understand why. Cities of ancient times, such as Jerusalem, were not built to be seen by others; they were built on high places in order to be more easily fortified and defended. Likewise, the lamp that is *set on a stand* is not placed there just to be seen. It shines quite naturally, because it is its nature to shine. Without pretense, it illuminates.

Therefore the Christian does not seek to be admired and to receive compliments. It is enough to be a Christian so as to please God and give him glory—so that, throughout our life, we might ask in the Lord's Prayer: "Hallowed be thy name." By acting in such loyal and disinterested way, but also in complete openness, the Christian gives witness that inspires other people to give glory to our heavenly Father. This happens when Christians understand, or at least suspect, that righteousness, peace, and charity have a source that is not entirely human.

If all of this is true for the individual Christian, it is even more true for the Christian home, which indeed is more than the combination of two individuals. Their communal witness is much stronger than the combined witness of two people because it is a witness of love and unity and the sharing of the same ideal.

You are the light of the world. Thus, because Jesus said the same thing about himself, "I am the light of the world" (Jn 9:5), Christians who have received the light of baptism reflect the light of Christ. They are "children of light" (Lk 16:8, Eph 5:8, 1 Thes 5:5). Also, the sacrament of confirmation enables us to witness Christ before the world.

That is why the two of you, who have been baptized and confirmed, are about to receive the sacrament of marriage. You will therefore build a home in which light will prevail, so that people will *give praise to your heavenly Father.*

3. THE HOUSE BUILT ON ROCK
(Mt 7:21, 24–29 [Long Form],
7:21, 24–25 [Short Form])

This pericope forms the conclusion of the Sermon on the Mount and has a corresponding passage in St. Luke (6:47–49). For our purposes, the differences between the two gospel recensions are negligible. Matthew's text contains the narrator's conclusion (7:28–29), which allows the evangelist to stress the force of Christ's words.

There is no apparent advantage in the short reading, for the complete text is not long. The strength of the parable is reinforced by the negative part that is suppressed in the short reading. Evidently, it would be regrettable to end a homily with the wrecking of the house. More precisely, verses 28 and 29 allow us to conclude with the strong affirmation that reinforces the lesson of the parable. It seemed to us that no purpose was served in placing in parentheses the ideas that pertain to these two verses.

As in the previous reading, the pericope is not directly related to marriage, but the image of a house being built quite naturally applies to the beginning of a home.

You have come here to be married to each other. Not only are you uniting yourselves as individuals, you are also beginning a home, a *house.* That is why the parable of the building of a *house on rock* was just read to you.

The parable is very clear. Nevertheless, to get an even better understanding of it we must call to mind some of the particulars about life in Palestine, the country of Jesus.

The homes of ordinary people were very modest in construction, with just one room and one door. The walls were thin and were made of clay. The root was a terrace, made of reeds that had been collected from the fields, and was haphazardly constructed, as were the walls (see Mt 24:43). The house might therefore collapse in the fall or spring, when violent winds and rain came in terrible storms from across the lake and flooded the dry ravines. The fragile houses could not resist such attacks, unless the builders had had the foresight to assure their solidity when they built them. They had to be careful not to build on sand, but on solid rock, which underlay much of Jesus' country.

It is easy to see how the parable applies to the home that you wish to begin today. You have many materials at your disposal for your task: your love, your hope, your good will, and your desire to be happily united to each other. But all of your materials are fragile, because—like all of us—you are simple, vulnerable creatures, exposed to the wear and tear of everyday life. Nor is everyday life the only problem. There are other problems and struggles that menace every person's life, and that are even more likely—if I may say so—in the life of a married couple. A husband and wife must overcome the bitterness of misunderstandings, the onset of unforeseen passions, and storms of trials, sorrows, and difficulties of every sort, both material and spiritual.

Not only are these dangers possible, they are predictable and inevitable. But you have no need to be frightened, provided you build your house on rock. The rock to which I refer is the strength of God's word and the strength of the faith by which you commit yourselves to that word.

Christ's doctrine, as taught to you by the Church, is not a human, hesitant word, or a simple opinion. It is not even a theology. It is stated in our gospel reading, which is the conclusion of Jesus' Sermon on the Mount: *Jesus finished this discourse and left the crowds spellbound by this teaching. The reason was that he taught with authority and not like their scribes.*

Therefore you have been instructed by God's word, because you have wanted to be married in church and because you have heard God's word proclaimed in the Sacred Scriptures, which I am explaining to you .

In order to build solidly on rock, it is not enough merely to voice approval of God's word. It is not enough to pray: *None of you who cry out, "Lord, Lord," will enter the kingdom of God. . . . Anyone who hears my words and puts them into practice is like the wise man who built his house on rock.* It is not enough to listen and speak. We must put Jesus' words into practice. You must put the doctrine, morality, and ideal of our gospel into practice every day of your life.

You, who are about to commit yourselves to each other, will indeed express your commitment with a word, but not simply a human word. Marriage is a sacrament, which means that your actions and your intention are supported by God. Marriage will create an indissoluble union between you. It will give you duties and responsibilities that you, and you alone, must accept. At the same time, marriage will provide you with grace, the help that God gives gratuitously and generously. We human beings can fall into the trap of merely talking and thereby fail to put our faith into practice. But it is not so with God. Whatever God says, he accomplishes.

It is not on a cold, inert rock that you build your home. It is on a living rock, on God, who will come to your aid to sustain and renew the determination of your will.

Go, then, with seriousness, but with complete confidence, as you undertake the construction of your home in such a way that it will resist every storm.

4. JESUS RATIFIES THE INDISSOLUBILITY OF MARRIAGE
(Mt 19:3–6)

6. LET NO ONE SEPARATE WHAT GOD HAS JOINED TOGETHER
(Mk 10:6–9)

Readings 4 and 6 are somewhat parallel; therefore their commentary is given in the homily proposed below. There is, however, an important difference in the readings. Matthew 19:3–6, as such, was the only gospel pericope in the marriage Mass of the old Roman Missal; that is why it has been retained intact in the new lectionary for marriage.

The duplication in Mk 10:6–9 allows us to omit the introduction (Mt 19:3 = Mk 10:2), in which "some Pharisees came up . . . to ask Jesus whether it was possible for a husband to divorce his wife" (Mk 10:2). In fact, it often happens that a marriage is celebrated before a crowd of people who have had divorces, even in the immediate families of the bride and groom. We can avoid embarrassment by using the passage from Mark.

Nevertheless, it is impossible to understand either gospel without some allusion to the question that was asked of Jesus. We cannot bring out the complete meaning in the passages unless we affirm the dogma of the indissolubility of marriage. Affirming the dogma in a sermon in which it has justification is less shocking than proclaiming a gospel that begins with the question of divorce.

We should indicate that Jesus' response, which high-
lights the two pericopes (Mt 19:4–5, Mk 10:6–8), brings
together two quotes from Genesis (Mt 19:4 and Mk 10:6
correspond to Gn 1:27; Mt. 19:5 and Mk 10:7–9 correspond to Gn 2:24). A closer examination of the two
Genesis texts can be found in the homilies provided for
Old Testament readings 1 and 2 (see pp. 17 & 20).

Therefore we should take the precaution to avoid
repetition by not using this gospel with one of the two
Genesis readings mentioned above. But if we decide to
use Mt 19 or Mk 10 with Gn 1 or Gn 2, we should state
that intention clearly, so that no one will judge that the
repetition is due to our negligence.

Nevertheless, it seems regrettable that two readings
in the Mass, and consequently the homily, might carry
only the theme of the indissolubility of marriage, a jurid-
ical reality that in itself is not very appealing. It would
be more fitting to complement this gospel, which deals
primarily with indissolubility, with an Old or New Testament reading that stresses the primacy of love.

We must not allow the Christian life to be controlled
by varying social pressures, customs, slogans of the time,
and the demands of routine conformity. I think that young
people who decide to marry in our day and age make their
decision in complete freedom, without concern for social
customs. I do not make this statement to advocate that
young people become capricious or live in a dream world.
Marriage is too serious for us to suggest anything like
that. A man and a woman in love need the eyes of faith
to discern the will of God as they accept a profoundly human moral imperative. The imperative, however, is quite
unconventional.

That is what we are reminded of in the gospel you
have heard. Some Pharisees wanted to lay a trap for Jesus;
this happened often and the trap was always the same.
They attempted to force Jesus to contradict the Law of

Moses. But Jesus had profound respect for the Mosaic law. He obeyed it in his personal life. In the Sermon on the Mount he solemnly declared that he came "not to abolish the law, but to fulfill it" (Mt 5:17).

Jesus absolutely refused to confuse the law that came from God with the human traditions that were added to the Law. And so the Pharisees came to ask Jesus about a practice that was tolerated by the Law of Moses. A married man could "repudiate" his wife for many motives, more or less serious, according to the rigorism or liberalism of the legal experts.

Here was the trap laid for Jesus: If he supported the indissolubility of marriage, as one might guess would be Jesus' opinion, based on his conduct and his preaching, he would have been condemned for despising the Law of Moses. If, on the other hand, he accepted the concessions admitted by the Law, he would be judged as placing himself in contradiction to the Law.

Jesus escaped the trap by rejecting the premise of his adversaries, whose argument was based on a more or less corrupt tradition, on a human practice that could be debated. Jesus appealed to God himself, whose will was described in Scriptures that were highly venerated and accepted by every Jew. Therefore Jesus cited two Genesis narratives on the creation of man and woman.

The first narrative states that in *the beginning* God wished to create a humanity consisting of men and women. The second narrative shows in a more exact manner how the woman was taken from the very flesh of the man. By nature, therefore, women are very close to men, and each experiences a deep attraction for the other.

Jesus was content with alluding to this text, which was very familiar to the men who were questioning him. He quoted the conclusion of the Genesis narrator: *For this reason,* because of the primordial will of the creator, *a man shall leave his father and mother and the two shall become as one. They are no longer two but one flesh.*

And so, in a way, marriage creates a new man. He is

separated from his original family and becomes the founder of another family. He clings to his wife in such an intimate manner, so totally and so definitively, that husband and wife become one person with one destiny. Previously, they had been two individuals, each with a separate place and vocation in society.

After giving the two reminders from Genesis, Jesus concluded with a personal statement: *Therefore, let no man separate what God has joined.*

It is not perfectly evident why Jesus made such a conclusion. Left to ourselves, we would not make a similar conclusion. But Jesus not only relies on the biblical word, he goes beyond it. By this last word, he completes divine revelation concerning marriage.

Surely each marriage is not immediately and exclusively the work of God. These future spouses have chosen each other freely. Marriage is the work of their will and depends on their decision. And that is why, in a few moments, I will ask the bride and groom to express their intention to be united to each other forever. Therefore we can correctly say that in a Christian marriage, as in a natural union, the spouses are the authors and the celebrants of their own union.

Even though marriage is a voluntary union in which the partners make a free choice, they are not thereby free to make of their union anything they want. In legal terms, their contract is inscribed in an institution. It is a natural institution, established by God in *the beginning*, when he created man and woman. Therefore every marriage, whether pagan or purely civil, is in itself indissoluble. But when there is a marriage between two baptized people, God intervenes in a more explicit and personal manner. The marriage of two baptized Christians is a great mystery, reflecting the marriage of Christ and the Church—that is, Christ's marriage with redeemed humanity. That is what St. Paul tells us when he quotes the same Genesis text that we have already heard confirmed by Jesus (Eph 5:31–32, New Testament reading 5).

Therefore, though you have freely chosen your union,

it is not any less the work of Christ and the work of God. It would be a desecration if God's work were to be destroyed by human inconsistency, capriciousness, selfishness, or stubbornness.

And so you will be united to one another, knowing that God himself is about to consecrate your union.

5. THE GREAT COMMANDMENT OF LOVE (Mt 22:35-40)

It must be constantly stated that there is a difficulty in commenting on readings that have *agape*, or love, or charity as their objective. We encountered this problem in the New Testament readings (numbers 1, 2, 4, 8, and 9) ; we face the same difficulty in the present gospel, and also in other Gospel readings (8, 9, and 10).

The word "love" is terribly equivocal. "Charity" has taken on the connotation of paternalistic good deeds, which also distorts the word *agape*. And so our commentary is complicated by the constant need to distinguish genuine love and genuine charity from counterfeit meanings. The significance of the two words is so devalued that "love" is overused and "charity" implies disgrace.

Nevertheless, though we distinguish these words, it is good to relate human love with divine love. It is also helpful to show that conjugal love is an eminent form of charity toward neighbors. This provides the opportunity for a teaching that will seem new and enriching for many of our listeners.

In the gospel you have just heard, Jesus summarizes his entire moral teaching, which is applicable to all his disciples. But the teaching does not seem to concern marriage in any special way.

I do not intend to restrict such a universal teaching of Jesus. Nevertheless, it is allowable for us to think that

our Lord's teaching has a special application today, because the reading hinges on the word "love" and because
marriage is the sacrament of love.

A specialist in Jewish law approached Jesus and asked
him: *What commandment of the law is the greatest?* This
was a classic question among rabbis, who tried to provide
clarity about practical application of all the commandments that comprised the law attributed to Moses. Let us
note that for us, too, the effort to simplify has value. According to some of the way in which Christian morality
is presented, this question can seem very detailed and
complicated.

This classic question, of an apparently elementary
nature, was a trick question when addressed to Jesus because it seemed to the rigorous Pharisees that Jesus was
relaxing the Law. Some examples can be cited: the precept of the sabbath (Lk 13:14, 14:3, Jn 5:9, 9:14), the
precept of washing one's hands for the ritual purification
before meals (Mk 7:1–13), and even the precept that pro-
hibited touching a leper, because of contamination (Mt
8:3). Jesus also went to the homes of pagans (Mt 8:7) and
made friends with sinners (Mt 8:11, Lk 7:39, 15:2).

Jesus avoided the trap by refusing to quote a specific
commandment of the Law. Instead, he gave a global precept, which was also attributed to Moses and to which
pious Jews were so attached that they repeated it several
times each day: "Hear, O Israel! The Lord our God is
Lord alone! *Therefore you shall love him with all your
heart, with all your soul, and with all your mind.*"[2] To
show that he has responded well to the question that was
posed to him, Jesus adds: *This is the greatest and first
commandment,* the foundation for all the other commandments.

Then Jesus adds a second commandment, also taken

2. Dt 6:5. We have quoted the beginning of the *Shemah Israel* as it
was given by our Lord in the parallel passage in Mk 12:29.

from the Mosaic precepts: *You shall love your neighbor as yourself.*[3]

The legal expert, who had approached Jesus, was quite familiar with this second commandment. Its association with the command to love God was not at all unheard of.

But Jesus demonstrates his boldness when he affirms that the command to love our neighbor is *like* the commandment to love God, to such an extent that the two commandments, in the last analysis, become but one commandment. That is precisely Jesus' conclusion: *On these two commandments the whole law is based, and the prophets as well.*

The unity, the quasi-identity between the two commandments, is of particular interest for us today. Let us suppose that I ask a question of the people who sit before me: "In all honesty, do you love God with all your heart, with all your soul, and with all your mind?" Their sincere response would not pass the test of conventional piety. "Well," they would say, "we must confess that for the moment it is not God but rather my spouse, my fiancé, that I love with all my heart, with all my soul, and with all my mind."

I would not at all be scandalized by such a reply. It is quite evident that love for the invisible God cannot rival in emotional intensity and affectionate attachment your love for the visible creature, whom you have chosen from among many, with whom you will be united for life, and from whom you expect your happiness. Your preference does not show any disdain for the commandment to love God above all things. Indeed, this engaged Christian couple knows very well that, in loving each other and in wanting to be united to each other before the Church, they are fulfilling a vocation that comes from God. They are obeying God and wish to give him glory through their love. I shall be so bold as to say that their love for God,

3. Lv 19:18.

which is a supreme but less tangible love, is incarnated in a much warmer human love.

That is so true. On several occasions St. Paul repeated our Lord's words by mentioning only the second commandment (which is like the first) without quoting the first commandment of love for God. He says, for example: "The whole law has found its fulfillment in this one saying: 'You shall love your neighbor as yourself' " (Gal 5: 14, also Rom 13:9) .[4]

You shall love your neighbor. And who is your neighbor? When a learned lawyer asked that question (Lk 10: 29) , Jesus replied with the parable of the Good Samaritan. And so our Lord taught us that "neighbor" means every person, especially those who are suffering most.

However, sincere charity must be universal and should exclude no one. Jesus urges only that we observe a certain order in our love. First and foremost, our neighbors are those who are closest to us: our parents, our friends, and the people we work with. But who is closer to the bride than her husband, and vice versa, since through marriage "they are no longer two but one flesh"? (See Gn 2:24, Old Testament reading 2; also see New Testament reading 7 and Gospel readings 4 and 6.) [5]

Loving your neighbor *as yourself.* This might seem difficult for most people, because they misunderstand the commandment. It does not mean to love your neighbor "as much as yourself" but "in the same manner." It means that we should not love people, who are God's sons and daughters, as our way of getting power and pleasure, which we seek only for ourselves and not for them. We must love others not as things but as persons, as persons who, like

4. We can also mention that the same thing occurs in Paul's eulogy of love (1 Cor 12:31–13:8). In that passage all the signs of genuine love, which is clearly theological charity in the strictest sense, directly concern the love of neighbor.

5. See the *Summa Theologica,* 2–2, quest. 26, art. 1, 3, 6, 7, 8.

us, have infinite value and are called by God to live for
all eternity.

With the exception of God, to whom we owe all that
we are, we cannot really love anyone more than ourselves.
The love that we have for ourselves is the root of every
other kind of love.[6] And when we consider that a man
and a woman are united through marriage to the point
that "the two shall become as one" person, it seems easy
to love the other person as oneself. This is what Paul ex-
pressly states with regard to the husband, and it is equally
true of the wife. He says: "Husbands should love their
wives as they do their own bodies. He who loves his wife
loves himself" (Gal 5:28, New Testament reading 5).

But love of this kind is very difficult and really goes
against our nature. A person can love foolishly by loving
in ways that are selfish, domineering, or at least condescending. Loving your spouse as yourself means to love
that person in an unselfish way, in a way that enables you
to make sacrifices. It means loving that person as someone
who is your equal, your partner, and your intimate friend.
In the same text, Paul gives a model of conjugal love
Christ's love for his Church, the love he has for the people
he has saved by immolating himself for them.

You need the graces that God will give you through
the sacrament of marriage precisely because God's love is
the source of love for neighbor and because Christ's love
for his Church is the model of conjugal love. Marriage
becomes the sacrament of your love only because it joins
your love to the love that Christ has for you.

6. Ibid., art 11.

6. LET NO ONE SEPARATE WHAT GOD HAS JOINED TOGETHER
(Mk 10:6-9)

This text closely parallels St. Matthew's passage, which is Gospel reading 4. See pp. 86-90 for the suggested homily that can be given for both of these closely related texts.

7. JESUS AND MARY AT THE WEDDING AT CANA
(Jn 2:1-11)

It can be said that St. John did not describe the miracle at Cana primarily to give a teaching on marriage. Jesus had just recruited his first disciples (Jn 1:35-51); now he draws them to himself with the first of the signs he was to perform: *Thus did he reveal his glory* [which is what "epiphany" means] *and his disciples believed in him* (Jn 2:11). As in many other episodes in the Fourth Gospel, the Cana miracle is related to Easter. Jesus makes his debut "on the third day" (after his call to Nathanael), which could hardly be stated by the lectionary at the beginning of our reading. *The hour* of Jesus is the hour of his Passover. Lastly, the narrative is followed by the remark: "The Jewish Passover was near" (Jn 2:13).

Nevertheless, it is quite natural to make some applications to marriage from the passage. To demonstrate their opposition to the rigorous sects that exaggerated an esteem of continence, all the Fathers of the Church stressed the gracious presence of Jesus and Mary at a marriage.

This gospel is the only one that allows us to reflect on the Virgin Mary's discreet request, which many Christian couples will appreciate. And because the gospel is a popular narrative, it can balance some of the first readings that are somewhat theoretical or remote.

There was a wedding feast at Cana in Galilee, and the mother of Jesus was there. She did not have to make a long trip, because Cana is only a few kilometers from Nazareth, her village. *Jesus and his disciples had likewise been invited to the celebration.* It should also be pointed out that Nathanael, one of the disciples, was from Cana (see Jn 21:2), and the description of his first encounter with Jesus (Jn 1:45–51) immediately precedes the narrative of the Cana wedding.

Except for the marriages mentioned in the parables, this is the only marriage described in the gospels. Jesus and his mother were invited, and they came. The Church has always considered this as proof that marriage was indeed willed by the creator. Marriage is "very good" (see Gn 1:31, Old Testament reading 1), a holy reality, a great and awesome mystery (see Eph 5:32, New Testament reading 5). However, marriage is not entirely a reality of this world, nor, from the Church's point of view, a last resort nor an unpleasant accommodation to human frailty.

Because you have come to be married in the Church, before the altar, to ask Jesus to be the primary witness and authority of your union, it is permissible that I apply to you the opening verse of our gospel: *There was a wedding feast . . . and the mother of Jesus was there. Jesus . . . had likewise been invited.*

The gospel does not describe a religious ceremony, and justifiably so, for a religious ceremony did not accompany a Jewish wedding. Its celebration was purely civil and took place in a family atmosphere. But we must add that because the Hebrew people were entirely consecrated to God, religion could never be absent from their lives. Fervent benedictions were addressed to God on behalf of the spouses.[7]

Our gospel speaks only of a wedding feast, and something happens: *They have no more wine.* This is serious, because, as the Bible often tells us, wine is both the sign

7. See R. De Vaux, *Ancient Israel: Its Life and Institutions* (London, 1961), pp. 33f., and Daniel-Rops, *Daily Life in the Time of Jesus* (New York, 1962), pp. 143ff.

and the source of joy. Will the wedding be overcast with sadness and boredom? Just then, Jesus works a miracle; he changes water into wine. And just as he came "that people might have life and have it in abundance" (Jn 10: 10) , he did not hesitate about performing a minor miracle. He transformed 600 liters of water into wine!

In the same generous manner, he would later multiply bread and fishes to feed thousands of his listeners in the desert, so that they were completely filled—so that the leftovers were collected in several bushels. All of these narratives insist on superabundance.

The Cana miracle is striking not only in its quantity but also in its quality. It is *choice wine,* and the *waiter in charge* seems to regret that it had not been served *first,* because *the guests have been drinking awhile* and may not fully appreciate the *choice wine!*

What is the significance of the generous and gracious miracle? Every Scripture commentator has pointed out that Christ provided the wine by means of the water that was *prescribed for Jewish ceremonial washing.* From this fact the commentators conclude that Jesus came to in- augurate a new covenant, a new testament—a change for the better. The old covenant was being perfected.

Jesus expressed his intentions in a clear manner: "I have not come to abolish . . . but to fulfill" the old Law (Mt 5:17) . He did not disdain the water, nor did he throw it out. On the contrary, he instructed that the water jars be filled to the brim. Then he transformed the water, which had been inert and tasteless. Jesus drew from it a drink that was warm, bracing, and joyful—from the wine the waiters drew from the jars *for Jewish ceremonial wash- ings.* Therefore the full revelation that Jesus brought is linked with God's word, which was already given through the Old Testament.

I believe that the transformation, innovation, and progress in quality that constitute Christianity are also found in marriage. Marriage is a reality of nature, created by God himself "at the beginning" of human history (Mt

19:4, Gospel reading 4; Mk 10:6, Gospel reading 6). Man
is created to be united to woman and to recognize in her
"the bone of his bone, and the flesh of his flesh" (Gn 2:
23, Old Testament reading 2). Mutual love is the basis of
their union, which is, of itself, a joyful thing. But marital
joy must become even more profound, even more delect-
able and durable, through the intervention of Jesus, who
makes of nature's law a "great mystery" of grace by trans-
forming human love with divine love.

But we can push the comparison even further. The
waiter in charge is astonished that such exquisite wine is
served when the meal is already well along. The custom
was that *people usually serve the choice wine first.* Even
Christians believe that a beginning is always more beautiful than what eventually will be accomplished. We dream
of a golden age, a lost paradise, "the good old days." With
regard to marriage, we glamorize the honeymoon.

In reality, it is not Christian to look backward. Christians must always look forward. We live with hope for
the future. We love progress and what lies ahead. We
know that Jesus is more ahead of us than behind us.

May you taste the *choice* wine of being faithful to the
grace of your marriage, until the end of your days together.
By the rule for quality wines, your marriage will become
even better as it ages!

In recalling the Cana miracle I have omitted an important, and (to be honest) somewhat disconcerting part
of the episode. I am referring to Mary's intervention.
Like a housewife concerned with serving her guests, she
foresaw the scarcity of wine. And as a loving mother, she
wanted to spare the young couple a cause for sadness and
disappointment. Therefore she made a request of her Son
in the most discrete manner. Without asking for anything,
she tells him: *They have no more wine.* Jesus responds
with a kind of refusal: *Woman, how does this concern of
yours involve me* Jesus calls her "woman" and not "mother" because he sees in her not only the person with
whom he has very tender ties but also the *woman* who

READINGS FROM THE FOUR GOSPELS

symbolizes and sums up all of humanity, the entire Church. That is way, at a solemn moment from the height of the cross, he would call out to her again: "Woman, there is your son" (Jn 19:26).

My hour has not yet come. What is Jesus' hour? That of his death and Resurrection, when he would open for redeemed humanity the font of life, love, and joy. It is the hour when the water and blood of new life and full joy, foreshadowed in the *choice wine* at Cana, would flow from the pierced heart of Jesus.

In the Cenacle, as his hour was approaching, Jesus performed a miracle that is even more beautiful than the Cana miracle. He changed the wine of the meal into his blood and gave it to us to drink.

In a few moments, you will be married. Fulfilling and continuing the Cana miracle, you too will drink from "the cup of the New Covenant."

We do not know whether Mary understood the meaning of Jesus' delay. But in the obscurity of her faith she had complete confidence in her Son as she said to the waiters: *Do whatever he tells you.* And so the miracle, apparently refused, is performed.

At a later time, at the foot of the cross, Mary would understand that her prayer went far beyond what she had first believed. Once she became Mother of the Church, represented by "the disciple whom Jesus loved," she would know that his hour had come. In the mystery of the wedding feast on the cross, Jesus would give sinful, restless, sorrowful people the fullness of joy that comes from the heart of the God who is love.

Indeed, Mary's prayer had been overextended—"overheard," if we can use that expression. This reminds me of a beautiful prayer that we say to God in the missal: "Your goodness is beyond what our spirit can touch and your strength is more than the mind can bear. Lead us to seek beyond our reach."[8]

8. From the 27th Sunday in Ordinary Time.

As you are joined in marriage before Jesus and his followers, who are gathered here, ask him for *choice wine,* with all the joy that it symbolizes. You will be heard through the intercession of the gentle Virgin Mary, provided you put into practice, throughout your entire life, her very simple but challenging advice: *Do whatever he tells you.*

8. LIVE ON IN MY LOVE
(Jn 15:9–13)

It seems appropriate that the awesome sublimity of the last three Johannine pericopes restricts them to the celebration of a marriage before a devout crowd, or at least to the celebration of marriage in a particularly fervent family. Such listeners will recognize the source of the pericopes.

However, the words that St. John ascribes to the remarks that Jesus makes to the eleven on Holy Thursday go beyond that chronological framework and have special importance for us today.

Although verses 12 and 13 of chapter 15 are found in Gospel readings 8 and 9, we have presented them in both contexts. These two verses play such different roles that our explanations will have to be modified accordingly.

The gospel we have chosen for your wedding Mass gives us an especially precious and serious teaching because it is from Jesus' farewell message to his disciples on the night before he died. In a certain sense, therefore, we are dealing with Jesus' last will and testament. As John tells us earlier in his gospel: Jesus "loved his own in the world" —that is, people who would continue to live in the world after his death—and showed that he loved them "to the end" (Jn 13:1). And so these final words are an invitation to love, or, more exactly, a promulgation of Jesus' law of love. This gospel is therefore a very appropriate reading for a wedding.

We immediately have a question. Are we dealing with the same kind of love? A famous painting by Titian represents "sacred love" and "profane love" side by side. Today, we would be inclined to title the painting. "Christian Charity and Secular Love" or, perhaps, "Supernatural Love and Natural Love." But such a distinction, or in any case their opposition, is debatable. Father Lacordaire once said: "There are not two loves."[9]

Surely we often apply the name "love" to something that does not deserve it: the sudden impulse of a moment, the desire to seek pleasure, the selfishness of two people. But the love that wants to give and offer itself, that seeks the other person for himself or herself and not for one's own pleasure, that finds joy in giving and making sacrifices—even when love exists between two human beings and even when it might be tainted by romance and sentimentality—yes, even this kind of love has God as its source and finds its model in Jesus.

Such love comes from God, because "God is love" (1 Jn 4:8, 16). The love flows from the Father to his Son, and from the Son to us: *As the Father has loved me, so I have loved you. Live on in my love.*

Let us emphasize the last sentence. Genuine love, love that comes from God and is blessed by God, is not a fleeting passion or a twenty-four hour fantasy. Real love is made to endure. That is why you have come to sanctify your love with a commitment before God, who will make of your commitment a union that will never be dissolved.

What is the necessary condition for continuing in love? Jesus tells us: *You will live in my love if you keep*

9. "My friend, there are not two loves; heavenly love and earthly love are the same, except insofar as heavenly love is infinite. When you wish to know what God is feeling, listen to the beating of your heart, and add only the infinite to what you hear." Lacordaire, *Lettres à des jeunes gens*, letter of July 5, 1838.

my commandments, even as I have kept my Father's commandments, and live in his love.

For us, there can seem to be opposition between *love* and *commandments*—as in Carmen's song: "Love is a carefree child, who has never, never known law."

Nevertheless, if love has a law, it is love's own law! God's commandments and Christ's commandments are not external constraints on love. On the contrary, they are the guarantees and signs of love. Real, durable, and faithful love, which is distinct from love that is no more than a passing sentiment or a simple heartthrob, proves itself through fidelity to commandments. Obedience to the commandments of love is itself a result of love. Obedience engenders love.

Jesus said: "He who obeys the commandments he has from me is the man who loves me; and he who loves me will be loved by my Father. I too will love him" (Jn 14:21). On that occasion Jesus was speaking of his commandments in the plural. But we must not see in his words a multiplying of minute and tyrannical prescripts. At the end of our gospel he speaks to us of just one commandment: *This is my commandment: love one another as I have loved you.*

The text is often quoted in an incomplete manner. When that happens, "love one another" seems to be a very commonplace invitation to good will and philanthropy. Jesus' complete quote is: *Love one another as I have loved you.* And to show how far love should go, Jesus immediately adds: *There is no greater love than this: to lay down one's life for one's friends.* Indeed, in just a few hours he will allow himself to be nailed to the cross through love for us.

You are not asked to submit to the humiliations and sufferings of the cross to demonstrate your love. But no doubt life has in store for you, as for everyone, many trials that will enable you to share in the cross of Jesus. What is really demanded of you is that you give your life. Yes, that is what marriage is all about. The sacrament of love implies a total, mutual gift of your lives to each other until death.

So as not to end an such an austere note, I have saved some words of Jesus that are more in harmony with today's celebration for the end of the homily: *All this I tell you that my joy may be yours and your joy may be complete.* Love of its very nature radiates joy. And the quality of joy depends on the quality of love. A coarse and whimsical love produces a dull and fragile joy. A profound and delicate love produces a profound and delicate joy. To the extent that love becomes perfect and roots itself in the trust of a life shared together, joy becomes more complete, more solid, and more genuine.

9. LOVE ONE ANOTHER AS I HAVE LOVED YOU
(Jn 15:12–16)

The words of Jesus that you have just heard are addressed to *his friends.* To be more precise, Jesus was speaking to the eleven Apostles, because the scene took place on Holy Thursday evening. The word "friends," however, has a broader meaning and can designate all those who wish to accept the teachings of our Lord. That means all baptized people, all Christians, yourselves.

Jesus spoke to them about what he calls *my command-ment,* a divine commandment that contains and surpasses all other commandments. Here is "the great command-ment," the commandment of love. Jesus calls it *my com-mandment* because he came to prescribe it to us with very definite insistence. He also came for the purpose of exem-plifying it for us: *This is my commandment: love one another as I have loved you.*

How have I loved you? You will see it in a few hours, when I will climb Calvary to give my life for you: *There*

*is no greater love than this: to lay down one's life for
one's friends.*

Therefore, because the commandment of love, fraternal charity, imposes an obligation on each Christian to love his brothers and sisters, what we more precisely call love, the relationship between husband and wife, is obviously an even greater realization of the commandment. In marriage, indeed, each spouse commits his life to the other and *lays down his life* for that person.

In another reading for the wedding Mass, St. Paul compares marriage to Christ's union with the Church, which means the human race, which he has saved through his sacrifice: "Husbands, love your wives, as Christ loved the Church. He gave himself up for her. . . . Husbands should love their wives as they do their own bodies" (Eph 5:25, 28, New Testament reading 5).

After his invitation to love with a generous and unselfish love, Jesus adds: *You are my friends if you do what I command you.* Therefore, should love be a question of obedience to a commandment? Should love be a duty or an enslavement, when all the while Jesus expects our hearts to be free and spontaneous? Not at all—because *this is my commandment* means to *love one another as I have loved you.* How can such a commandment be obeyed unless a person loves? But why *is* there such a commandment? Isn't love sufficient?

Love would be enough if we were perfectly pure, upright, and infallible creatures. But all of us by nature, or rather as a consequence of sin, are caught up with selfishness and the desire for pleasure. It is necessary that we love each other *as I have loved you.* Such generous love is not easy to observe without yielding to alteration or fatigue. We must therefore remain faithful to the commandment, whatever the cost may be.

There is no question here of slavish obedience. Jesus immediately speaks to us in clear terminology: *I no longer speak of you as slaves, for a slave does not know what his master is about. Instead, I call you friends, since I have made known to you all that I have heard from my Father.*

Let us go even further in clarifying Jesus' words. Christians do not "externally" obey a commandment that is imposed from outside, a commandment that "bullies" their freedom. They obey the commandment of love and they do so through love, with the help of grace—that is, by sharing in God's intimate life. Grace makes Christians deeply sympathetic and spontaneously in accord with what is pleasing to God.

When we obey someone we love by doing what pleases him, we are actually doing what is pleasing to ourself. Therefore, one is no longer acting only on obedience; one is doing what one wishes. In this light, St. Augustine's imperative may be easy to understand: "Love and do whatever you wish," because what you wish is pleasing to the person you love.

In the gospel, our Lord pointed out two essential attributes of friendship: intimacy and trust. Contrary to what we might often believe, the two attributes are also applicable to love, as all true love, and particularly conjugal love, is friendship. Although the word "friendship" has a weaker connotation than "love," with regard to total attachment and unity "friendship" suggests what is perhaps the most delicate flower of genuine love and conjugal love: a sharing of life in equality and harmony, a continuing intimacy, and a trust that remains constant day after day.

As we celebrate your marriage, we ask God for all the gifts that have been mentioned. In other words, we ask for all the gifts that constitute the grace of the sacrament of marriage, the sacrament of deep love in the closest friendship.

According to an easily understood gospel saying, the grace of marriage must *bear fruit*. This is what Jesus said. The quote that I am about to give primarily concerns the disciples to whom Jesus addressed it. Primarily, Jesus was considering their vocation and, secondarily, their missionary task and its fruits in terms of conversions. And yet we must not forget that, just as there is a vocation to the apostolate and the resultant fruits, there is also a vocation to marriage, with the grace and fruits of marriage. The comparison between the apostolate and marriage allows me to address Christ's words also to you: *It was not you who chose me, it was I who chose you* (marriage is a departure toward an entirely new life) and *I chose you to go forth and bear fruit. Your fruit must endure.*

The image of bearing fruit is related to the parable of vine that Jesus proposed earlier in the gospel (Jn 15: 1–11). Fruit is also an image of the productivity that flows from unity. For the Jews, the fruitful vine suggested a prosperous home and the mother of a blessed family, as is sung in one of the marriage psalms (Ps 128). Richness and joy are also symbolized, because the vine gives us wine "that cheers men" (Jgs 9:13). The fruits of the vine are evidently the children in whom the married couple is multiplied through its unity. Fruit is also the complete apostolic, human, charitable, and friendly radiance that is part of the vocation of Christian family life.

This magnificent ideal will be supported by prayer, a prayer that we can be confident is heard by those who know that in their union and throughout their lives they are doing the will of the Father: *So that all you ask the Father in my name he will give you.*

And so we are about to witness the commitments that you will express to each other. We will pray to the Father with confidence that, in Christ's name, we will be heard.

10. MAY THEIR UNITY BE COMPLETE
(Jn 17:20–26 [Long Form], 20:20–23 [Short Form])

Our suggested homily concerns only the verses that constitute the short reading. In fact, verses 24–26, which follow in the long form, are very beautiful and deep, but they are difficult to comment on. "These verses are not only a continuation of the preceding verses but also the conclusion of the entire prayer" (from La Grange in C. Spicq's *Agape in the New Testament,* 3:80). The three verses, in our opinion, do not contain a new theme for a wedding homily.

The gospel fragment, which you have just heard, is part of the very powerful prayer spoken by Jesus in the context of the Last Supper. But we would be mistaken if we regard the passage as only a touching memory that is buried in the past, as pertaining only to the eleven Apostles who surrounded Jesus at that moment. In fact, Jesus states very clearly: *I do not pray for them alone. I pray also for those who will believe in me through their word.*

At that very moment, Jesus considered us; he had us in his thoughts. He prayed for people who, many centuries later, would receive the word of the Apostles and their successors. He thought of all the people who were to receive the "good news" and the Church's teaching and who would believe in him as Jesus, the Savior, the divine Son of God. Yes, at that moment Jesus was thinking of us and praying for us.

What did Jesus ask on our behalf? He asked for unity: *that all may be one.* All the faithful, all members of the Church of whom it would be correctly said, a little after his departure into heaven: "The community of believers were of one heart and one mind" (Acts 4:32). It is in line with the prayer of Jesus that we pray for the unity of the Church, the reconciliation of Christians, and world peace.

But today, as we celebrate a marriage, we are also correct in giving Christian unity a more exact meaning, because we learn from the first book of the Bible, Genesis, which Jesus quoted at another time: "A man . . . clings to his wife, and the two of them become one body" (Gn 2:24, Old Testament reading 2; Eph 5:31, New Testament reading 5; Mt 19:5–6, Gospel reading 4; Mk 10:8, Gospel reading 6). And Jesus added: "Therefore let no man separate what God has joined!" (Mk 10:9).

In the preceding verses Jesus said something quite extraordinary. The union of man and woman is not only willed and accomplished by God, but something more is involved. Because your marriage is a Christian marriage and because your love is a love of charity, your marital unity is the image of the unity that exists between God the Father and his Son, Jesus Christ. Our faith recognizes that the Father and Jesus are two Persons, but, as we say in the Credo at Mass, "We believe in one God . . . Jesus Christ, true God from true God . . . one in Being with the Father" (Nicene Creed). Therefore Jesus prays: *That all may be one, as you, Father, are in me, and I in you; I pray that they may be [one] in us.* What is the glory that the Father has given to Jesus? And can Jesus really give the same glory to his human creatures?

In the Bible, "glory" does not mean the fame or renown of great political figures and superstars. Glory is one of God's names, a name that attempts to suggest the fullness of his being, the burst and flash of his light, the radiance of his infinite goodness. Jesus will be in the Father's glory after his Resurrection. But even before his Resurrection, as soon as "the Word became flesh," when Jesus came among us as a man, we saw "his glory: the glory of an only Son coming from the Father" (Jn 1:14). By his goodness and power, which are manifested in his miracles, Jesus is a reflection of the Father, as a reflection in a mirror. He would say to one of his disciples: "Whoever has seen me has seen the Father. . . . I am in the Father and the Father is in me" (Jn 14:9, 11).

In fact, we share in the divine nature that is equally in the Father and in Jesus. We are Christians through baptism, which brought us into the intimacy of the divine Persons. What we call grace is what Jesus, in a less full but very real manner, gives us: the glory that the Father has given him.

Grace is an invisible reality, but glory, on the other hand, makes us think of a kind of radiance. Indeed, Jesus tells us today that the unity that originates in the Father and Jesus, the unity that is realized among Christians, is an invitation to faith for those who witness it.

You are thinking, no doubt, that you are being united especially for your happiness. That is true. But you must not believe that your union, destined to become a perfect union, concerns you alone. Because it is a union inspired by both human and divine charity, it is impossible that charity, unselfish love, will not be transformed in the eyes of the people who will frequent your home, be warmed by its joy, and grow in its peacefulness.

Among Christians, genuine unity and genuine love emanate from God's love. More convincing than anything else in human experience, authentic love is a discrete but powerful proof that there is a God—a God who is love, a God who loves us, a God in whom Christians love each other. This is especially true in the case of married people, who have transformed their love into a sign and reflection of divine love.

Thus Jesus concludes this part of his very powerful prayer: *That their unity may be complete. So shall the world know that you sent me, and that you loved them as you loved me.*